THE CONFLICTS BETWEEN THE COMPANIONS
AND THE POSITION OF THE PIOUS PREDECESSORS REGARDING THEM

Publisher:
Umm-ul-Qura Publications
Fattomand Gujranwala
Pakistan
Website: www.umm-ul-qura.org
E-mail: khan_ali_hassan@hotmail.com

Cover design and typesetting by www.ihsaandesign.com

THE CONFLICTS BETWEEN THE COMPANIONS

AND THE POSITION OF THE PIOUS PREDECESSORS REGARDING THEM

BY SHAYKH IRSHAD AL-HAQQ AL-ATHARI

Translated by Ali Hassan Khan

Umm-ul-Qura Publications

TABLE OF CONTENTS

TRANSLATOR'S INTRODUCTION

All praises belong to Allah, the Lord of the universe!

It is a great honour for Umm-ul-Qura Publications to translate this book of Shaykh Irshad Al-Haqq Athari who introduced many of our books in Urdu such as *Maqalat Muhadith Gondalwi, Maqalat Hadith* of Shaykh Isma'eel Salafi, and *Difa Sahih Al-Bukhari* of Shaykh Abul Qasim Sayf Banarsi. Also the noble Shaykh gave us the permission to publish his Tahqiq of *I'lam Ahlil Asr bi Ahkam Rak'atay Al-Fajr* of Allamah Azeemabadi to which Hafiz Shahid Mahmood added another epistle of Shaykh Irshad Al-Haqq Athari on this topic after getting it translated into Arabic. Likewise Shaykh Irshad Al-Haqq Al-Athari allowed us to translate into Arabic and publish his books *I'la Sunnan fil Mizan* and *Asbab Ikhtilaf Fuqaha* and they were thus printed under the supervision of Hafiz Shahid Mahmood.

The translation of this book was much needed as some popular speakers in Pakistan having a large following on social media started to raise objections to the noble companions and especially against Mu'awiyah ﷺ, affecting the minds of many laymen.

I have added some footnotes to this book preceded by the letter "Tr"; I have taken the English translation of the Quran mostly from the translation of "Saheeh International" and also taken some translations of Ahadith from translated sources.

I pray to Allah ﷻ to make this book beneficial and give us the Tawfeeq to translate further books of Shaykh Irshad Al-Haqq Athari and others from our great scholars.

May Allah send Salah and Salam on the Prophet ﷺ, his household and companions!

BIOGRAPHY OF THE AUTHOR

Shaykh Muhammad Ishaq Bhatti mentioned in *Gulistan Hadith* (p458) that in 1968, Shaykh Abdullah Lailpuri and Shaykh Muhammad Ishaq Cheemah called a meeting between some scholars in which Shaykh Muhammad Haneef Nadwi requested Shaykh Bhatti to join them. The six scholars who met were Shaykh Abdullah Lailpuri, Shaykh Ishaq Cheemah, Shaykh Muhammad Abduh Falah, Hafiz Ahmadullah Budhimalvi, Shaykh Haneef Nadwi and Shaykh Bhatti. The aim of this meeting was that Shaykh Muhammad Ishaq Cheemah wanted to establish an institute for graduate students to study further and specialise by studying higher books. Shaykh Haneef Nadwi advised him to call this institute "Idarah Ulum Athariyah" so that those who study from there will be called "Athari" and this attribution is the authentic symbol of our school of thought. Shaykh Ishaq Bhatti was requested to write the aim of this institute and all scholars agreed on his writing.

Shaykh Irshadul Haqq Athari studied in the "Idarah Ulum Athariyah" after having completed his Dars Nizami, and he is today the director of "Idarah Ulum Athariyah".

Shaykh Irshad Al-Haqq Al-Athari was born in 1948. His father's name was Ghulam Rasool and he resided in Chak No. 72-7 Aare, Tahseel Faqeer Wali (in the area of Bahawal Nagar). When Shaykh Irshad Al-Haqq was two years old, his father moved to Chak No. 24 Liaqatpur. His father had studied up to middle school, he would recite the Quran regularly and pray Tahajudd and was constantly involved in the remembrance of Allah. His family were all Barelwi but through his reading of books of Shaykh Mawdudi and linking himself to the scholars of Deoband, Shaykh Irshad Al-Haqq's father became attached to the Deobandi school of thought.

When Shaykh Irshad Al-Haqq Al-Athari reached the age of discernment, his father enrolled him to a middle school in Liaqatpur. In 1961, he underwent the mid-exams and read the Quran from Molvi AbdulHafeez. Afterwards, he joined the Madrasah "Qasim Al-Ulum" in Liaqatpur. He studied beginner books from Shaykh Muhammad Basheer and Shaykh Muhammad Hayat, books of Persian, Arabic grammar and morphology, the Hanafi book of Fiqh *Al-Quduri* and the book of Mantiq *Taysir Al-Mantiq*, and these studies took two years.

His teachers advised his father that for further studies, his son should go to "Madrasah Qasim Al-Ulum" in Faqeer Wali or "Jamiyah Rasheediyah" in Montgomery or "Khayr Al-Madaris" in Multan, but his father was not ready to send him that far. At the time Mufti AbdurRahman arrived in Liaqatpur and Shaykh Irshad Al-Haqq Athari's father joined his circle. Mufti AbdurRahman was a class fellow of Shaykh Sharifullah Khan in the "Madrasah Fathpur" in Delhi and at this time Shaykh Sharifullah Khan, a reputed Hanafi scholar, was a teacher in "Jamiyah Salafiyah Faisalabad", so Mufti AbdurRahman advised Shaykh Irshad Al-Haqq Athari's father to send his son to "Jamiyah Salafiyah". His father accepted this advice as his sister and other family members were living in Nurpur, near the Jamiyah. Also among the reasons was that Shaykh Irshad Al-Haqq's father had visited Jamiyah Salafiyah and obtained spiritual tranquillity (Ruhani Taskeen) after visiting Hafiz Muhammad Gondalwi who was the Shaykh Al-Hadith of Jamiyah Salafiyah at the time, so he thought that his son would benefit a lot from such a great scholar, and hence he accepted the advice of Mufti AbdurRahman.

Shaykh Irshad Al-Haqq Athari joined "Jamiyah Salafiyah Faisalabad" in 1964, and at this time he was Hanafi. He studied from Hafiz Abdullah Budhimalvi, Peer Muhammad Ya'qub Jhelumi, Shaykh Sadiq Khalil, Shaykh Muhammad Haneef Salafi, Hafiz Muhammad Binyameen, Shaykh Abdullah Amjad and others. During his studies, sometimes he would discuss topics of Fiqh with other students but always with respect and none of his teachers pressured him to change his school of thought, but when he started his third year of studies, through his own research and reading, especially the books of Shaykh AbdurRahman Mubarakpuri, he opted for the Ahl-e-Hadith school of thought.

Shaykh Irshad Al-Haqq Athari studied for three years in "Jamiyah Salafiyah", but due to some reasons Hafiz Muhammad Binyameen left the Jamiyah and went to teach in Katto, so Shaykh Irshad Al-Haqq with other students went there as well, where he studied there *Sahih Muslim, Abu Dawud, Daraqutni* and others from Hafiz Muhammad Binyameen.

In 1968, Shaykh Irshad Al-Haqq Athari joined "Jamiyah Islamiyah" in Gujranwala, and he studied from Hafiz Muhammad Gondalwi and Shaykh Abul Barakat Ahmad and obtained his Sanad of completion.

In 1969, he joined "Idarah Ulum Athariyah" in Faisalabad and studied there from Shaykh Abdullah Lailpuri and Shaykh Muhammad Abduh Falah. Shaykh Irshad Al-Haqq Athari had a great fervour to read books and research, hence after his studies he became attached to "Dar Ulum Athariyah" and decided to reside permanently in Faisalabad. He is presently director of this Dar Ulum.

HIS WRITINGS

ARABIC WORKS

1) *Al-Ilal Al-Mutanahiyah fil Ahadith Al-Wahiyah li Ibn Jawzi*: Shaykh Irshad Al-Haqq Athari did Tahqiq of this famous book of Imam Ibn Jawzi which contains weak and fabricated narrations by comparing two manuscripts of it and it was published in 1979 in two volumes for the first time. It was published by Idarah Ulum Athariyah in partnership with Islamic Publishing House Lahore.

2) *I'lam Ahlil Asr bi Ahkam Rak'atay Al-Fajr* of Shaykh Shamsul Haqq Azeemabadi: This is a famous book of Shaykh Azeemabadi in Arabic on the rulings of the two Rak'ah of Fajr. Shaykh Athari republished it with his Tahqiq and notes in 1394 by Idarah Ulum Athariyah. Umm-ul-Qura Publications published this work again recently and added to it an epistle of Shaykh Irshad Al-Haqq Athari on the same topic, after translating it from Urdu to Arabic under the supervision of Hafiz Shahid Mahmood.

3) *Musnad Imam Abi Ya'la Al-Mawsuli*: Shaykh Irshad Al-Haqq Athari did Tahqiq and Takhrij of this book of Hadith of Imam Abu Ya'la Ahmad ibn Ali ibn Muthana Al-Mawsuli (d. 307 AH) and it was published for the first time by Maktabah Dar Al-Qiblah li Thaqafah Al-Islamiyah Jeddah in six volumes. Shaykh Faydh Ar-Rahman Thawri joined him in this task up to approximately the first half of the book.

4) *Kitab Al-Mu'jam* of Imam Abu Ya'la Al-Mawsuli: Shaykh Irshad Al-Haqq Athari did Tahqiq of this book by Imam Abu Ya'la. It was published for the first time in 1407 AH by Idarah Ulum Athariyah.

5) *Jala Al-Aynayn bi Takhrij Riwayat Al-Bukhari fi Juzz Rafil Yadayn*: This was the Arabic book of Shaykh Badiudin Shah Rashdi; Shaykh Irshad Al-Haqq verified the book and added some notes to it from the copy of Shaykh Faydh Ar-Rahman's Thawri's Tahqiq of *Juzz Rafil Yadayn*. This book was published by Idarah Ulum Athariyah in 1983 and Shaykh Salahdin Maqbool Ahmed published it afterwards in Kuwait by Dar Al-Gheras.

6) *Fadhail Shahr Rajab* of Imam Abu Muhammad Al-Hasan ibn Muhammad Al-Khallal Al-Baghdadi (d 439). Shaykh Irshad Al-Haqq Athari did Tahqiq and Takhrij of this epistle.

7) *Tabyin Al-Ujab bima Warada fi Fadhl Rajab* of Hafiz Ibn Hajar Asqalani. Shaykh Irshad Al-Haqq did Taqhqiq and Takhrij of this epistle and it was published together with the previous epistle of Imam Khallal by Idarah Ulum Athariyah in 1994.

8) *Al-Maqalah Al-Husna fi Sunniyah Al-Musahafah bil Yad Al-Yumna*: This was an Urdu epistle of Shaykh AbdurRahman Mubarakpuri on the Sunnah of shaking the hands with the right hand. It was translated from Urdu to Arabic by Shaykh Wasiullah Abbas and Shaykh Irshad Al-Haqq Athari did Tahqiq of it and published it under Idarah Ulum Athariyah.

9) *Musnad As-Siraj*: This is the Musnad of Imam Muhammad ibn Ishaq As-Siraj An-Nisapuri (d. 313 AH). The complete manuscript of it is lost and only a part of it is present in Maktabah Zahiriyah in Damascus. Shaykh Irshad Al-Haqq Athari published it for the first time in 2002 with his Tahqiq and Takhrij by Idarah Ulum Athariyah in a single volume of 496 pages.

10) *Ta'qeeb ala At-Taqreeb*: These are notes of Shaykh Irshad Al-Haqq on *Taqreeb At-Tahzib* of Hafiz Ibn Hajar and he added narrators which fall under the conditions of *Taqreeb*. It was published by Dar An-Nashar Al-Kutub Al-Islamiyah Lahore in 1985.

11) *Al-Ahadith Al-Eediyah Al-Musalsalah*: It is the epistle of Imam Abu Tahir Ahmad ibn Muhammad As-Silafi Al-Asbahani, Shaykh Irshad Al-Haqq Athari did Tahqiq and Takhrij of it and it was published in 2008 by Dar Al-Bashair Al-Islamiyah Kuwait in 63 pages.

12) *Ghayah Al-Maqsad fi Zawaid Al-Musnad Imam Ahmad*: This is the book of Hafiz Nurudin Ali Ibn Abi Bakr Al-Haythami (d. 807 AH) in which he gathers all the narrations of *Musnad Imam Ahmad* which are not present in the *Sihah Sittah* (the six famous books of Hadith) or are present with additions in the Musnad. Shaykh Irshad Al-Haqq Athari did Tahqiq and Takhrij of this book and it has been published by Maktabah Bayt As-Salam Riyadh in four volumes with the introductions of Shaykh Wasiullah Abbas, Shaykh Abul Ashbal Sagheer Ahmad Saghif and Shaykh Ozair Shams. Maktabah Bayt As-Salam is the Maktabah of Hafiz Abid Elahi Zaheer, the younger brother of Allamah Ihsan Elahi Zaheer.

13) *Majalis Al-Abrar*: This is a book of Allamah Turki, Shaykh Irshad Al-Haqq Athari did Tahqiq and Takhrij of it and it was published by Suhail Academy Lahore.

14) *Itmam Al-Manfa'ah bi Ta'jeel Al-Manfa'ah*: This book of Hafiz Ibn Hajar contains the narrators which are not in *Tahzib At-Tahzib* from those whom the four Imams narrated: the narrators of *Muwatta Malik, Musnad Imam Abu Hanifah, Musnad Imam Shafi'i* and *Musnad Imam Ahmad*. But Hafiz Ibn Hajar missed many of those narrators who fall under such conditions and Shaykh Irshad Al-Haqq Athari added in this book 260 narrators with their Tarjamah to complete Hafiz Ibn Hajar's book. It was published by Idarah Ulum Athariyah with the introduction of Shaykh Abul Ashbal Ahmad Shaghif in 184 pages. Shaykh Irshad Al-Haqq Athari's student Hafiz Muhammad Khubaib Ahmed helped him in this work.

15) Takhrij of *Izalah Al-Khafa 'an Khilafah Al-Khulafah*: This famous book of Shah Waliyullah Muhadith Dehlwi was written in Persian to refute the doubts raised by the Shi'a on the first three caliphs. Shaykh Muhammad Basheer Sialkoti translated it into Arabic and published it under Dar Al-Ilm Islamabad in two large volumes with the Takhrij of Shaykh Irshad Al-Haqq Athari.

16) *Ila As-Sunnan fil Mizan*: This book was originally written in Urdu refuting some principles of Hadith of Shaykh Zafar Ahmad Thanvi in his book *I'la As-Sunnan*. This was book was translated into Arabic under the supervision of Hafiz Shahid Mahmood and published by Umm-Ul-Qura Publications in 436 pages with the introductions of Shaykh Suhaib Hasan AbdulGhaffar and Shaykh Muhammad Ozair Shams. It was published afterwards by Maktabah Bayt As-Salam Riyadh.

17) *Asbab Ikhtilaf Al-Fuqaha*: This book was originally written in Urdu refuting the book *Athar Al-Hadith Ash-Sharif* by Shaykh Muhammad Awwamah and it was translated into Arabic under the supervision of Hafiz Shahid Mahmood and published by Umm-ul-Qura Publications with an article of Shaykh Irshad Al-Haqq translated as well in Arabic on the issue of the narration in *Mussanaf Ibn Abi Shaybah* on putting the hands below the navel, refuting the verification of Shaykh Muhammad Awwamah. This Arabic translation was introduced by Shaykh Salahdin Maqbool Ahmed. It was published afterwards by Bayt As-Salam Riyadh.

18) Shaykh Irshad Al-Haqq Athari's Urdu book *Mushajarat Sahabah or Salaf ka Mawqif* has also been translated in Arabic by Shaykh Rashid Hasan Mubarakpuri in India.

URDU WORKS

19) *Imam Daraqutni*: This is a biography of Imam Abul Hasan Ali ibn Umar Daraqutni and it contains the names of his 62 books with a brief description of them. This was the first book written by Shaykh Irshad Al-Haqq Athari and it has recently been reprinted within the Shaykh's Maqalat with additions in Maqalat volume five.

20) *Sihah Sittah or un ke Mualifin*: This was the first book published by Idarah Ulum Athariyah and most of it was due to the efforts of Shaykh Irshad Al-Haqq

21) *Qadiyanu Kafir Kiyun*: A 127 page book against Qadianism.

22) *Masalah Raful Yadayn par Ek Nai Kawish ka Jaizah* also called *At-Tahqiq wal Idah li Labs ma fi Nur As-Sabah*. This book refutes new evidences presented in the book *Nur As-Sabah* on not raising hands before and after Ruku. Shaykh Irshad Al-Haqq Al-Athari wrote this book on the request of Shaykh Ata'ullah Haneef Bhujiyani and it was printed by Dar Ad-Da'wah Salafiyah in 1981.

23) *Tawdih Al-Kalam fi Wujub Qira'ah Khalf Al-Imam*: This book in 1032 pages is a reply to *Ahsan Al-Kalam* of Shaykh Sarfraz Khan Safdar, on the obligation to recite Surah Fatihah behind the Imam.

24) *Tanqih Al-Kalam fi Tayid Tawdih Al-Kalam*: This is a 392 page book which replies to the book *Tawdih Al-Kalam par ek Nazar* which was authored by Shaykh Habibullah Derwi, a student of Shaykh Sarfraz Khan Safdar, and in which Shaykh Derwi levelled objections against the book *Tawdih Al-Kalam*.

25) *Pakohind mein Ullama Ahl e Hadith ki Khidmat Hadith*: This is a 144 page book on the efforts of the Ahl-e-Hadith in Hadith.

26) *Asbab Ikhtilaf Fuqaha*: A 128 page book refuting *Athar Al-Hadith Sharif* of Shaykh Muhammad Awammah.

27) *Ahadith Hidayah, Fanni wa Tahqiqi Haythiyat*: 112 page book mentioning some weak and fabricated Ahadith in the Hanafi book of Fiqh *Al-Hidayah*.

28) *Ahadith Sahih Bukhari or Muslim Mein Perwezi Tashkik ka Ilmi Jaaizah*: A 224 page book refuting Perwezis' objections against many Ahadith in the *Sahihayn*, and as well some of Shaykh Habib Ar-

Rahman Kandhelwi's rejection of some Ahadith due to his rationalist tendencies.

29) *Molana Sarfraz Safdar Apni Tasanif ke Ainah mein*: A 278 page book showing some mistakes and contradictions of Shaykh Sarfraz Safdar Khan in many of his books.

30) *Ainah un ko Dekhaya to Bura Man Gaye*: When Shaykh Irshad Al-Haqq Athari showed contradictions in the books of Shaykh Sarfraz Khan Safdar, his son wrote a reply entitled *Majzubanah Wa Wela*, and Shaykh Irshad Al-Haqq replied to him in this book.

31) *Imam Bukhari par Ba'd Itirazat ka Jaaizah*: A 126 page book in reply to some criticism of Shaykh Habeebullah Derwi on some Ahadith of *Sahih Bukhari*. After Shaykh Irshad Al-Haqq had shown the status of Ahadith in the book *Hidayah*, Shaykh Habeebullah Derwi in reply tried to criticise some narrations in *Sahih Al-Bukhari*.

32) *Afat e Nazar or un ka Ilaj*: A 95 page book on the evil eye and how to cure from it.

33) *Maslak Ahnaf or Molana Abul Hai Lukhnawi*: This 160 page book showing dozens of cases in which Shaykh Abdul Hai Lukhnawi left the Hanafi Madhab and chose to act upon Hadith.

34) *Mushajarat Sahabah or Salaf ka Mawqif*: A 120 page book showing the position of the Salaf on the conflicts between the companions. This book is now in your hands.

35) *Falah ki Rahein*: This 192 page book explains the first 11 verses of Surah Mu'minun.

36) *Piyare Rasul ki Piyari Namaz*: A small book describing the prayer of the Prophet ﷺ.

37) *Islam or Musiqi, Shubuhat wa Mughaltat ka Izalah*: A 136 page showing that Music is forbidden and refuting some doubts regarding it.

38) *Islam or Musiqi par Ishraq ke Itiradhat ka Jaaizah*: Refutation of some objections raised in the magazine *Ishraq* and by Ahmed Javed Ghamdi on music.

39) *Maqam Sahabah*: 173 pages on the noble status of the Companions.

40) *Tafsir Surah Qaf*: 200 pages.

41) *Tafsir Surah Fatir*: 323 pages

42) *Tafsir Surah Yaseen*: 442 pages

43) *Tafsir Surah As-Safat*: 456 pages

44) *Ila As-Sunnan fil Mizan*: 432 pages refuting the principles of Hadith of Shaykh Zafar Ahmed Thanvi in his *I'la As-Sunnan*. This book does not discuss topics of jurisprudence but only principles of Hadith.

45) *Sharh Hadith Ibn Abbas*: 175-page explanation of the famous Hadith in which the Prophet ﷺ advised Abdullah ibn Abbas ﷺ.

46) *Dhawabit Jarh wa Ta'deel*: A 118 page book compiled by Hafiz Muhammad Yunus Athari from a series of lectures of Shaykh Irshad Al-Haqq Athari on principles of Jarh wa Ta'deel. This book was published by "Al-Madinah Islamic Research Centre" Karachi.

47) *Hirz Al-Mumin*: A small pocketsize 80 page booklet on invocations, published by Idarah Ulum Athariyah.

48) *Maqalat* in five volumes: These include all the articles of Shaykh Irshad Al-Haqq Athari in *Al-Itisam* and others on diverse issues such as jurisprudence, history, biographies, principles of Hadith, creed and other topics.

49) *Maqalat Mubarakpuri*: It contains many Urdu epistles of Shaykh AbdurRahman Mubarakpuri, upon which Shaykh Irshad Al-Haqq Athari and his student Hafiz Muhammad Khubaib Ahmed added some notes.

50) Tahqiq and notes on *Al-Amr Al-Mubram li Ibtal Al-Kalam Al-Muhkam* of Shaykh Abul Qasim Sayf Banarsi, which has been included in *Difa Sahih Bukhari* by Hafiz Shahid Mahmood who compiled all the epistles of Shaykh Abul Qasim Banarsi written against the Hanafi Umar Kareem Patni who attacked *Sahih Al-Bukhari*.

The Shaykh Irshad Al-Haqq Athari has reviewed many books including:

a) The Urdu translation of *Bulugh Al-Maram* with the explanation of Shaykh SafiurRahman Mubarakpuri in two volumes printed by Darussalam.

b) The Arabic text of Ahadith in *Zia Al-Kalam fi Sharh Umdah Al-Ahkam* of Shaykh Mahmood Ahmad Ghadanfar.

c) The Seerah Encyclopaedia published by Darussalam in 11 volumes entitled *Al-Lulu Al-Maknun*, which is now being translated into English; the first volume has been printed.

d) *Gustakh Rasul ki Saza or us ka Anjam* of Shaykh Muhammad Zubair, published by Maktabah Islamiyah.

HIS OTHER SERVICES

The Shaykh, along with his research and writing, has also been teaching in "Markaz Tarbiyah Al-Islamiyah" Faisalabad established by Hafiz Muhammad Shareef and he has been very active lecturing in Pakistan and around the world.

From 1998 to 1999, Shaykh Irshad Al-Haqq Al-Athari was member of the Islami Nazriyati Council (Islamic Ideological Council) which is a governmental body whose aim is to scrutinise the bills presented in parliament on whether they are conform to the Book and the Sunnah. Shaykh Irshad Al-Haqq Athari has occupied the following different positions:

a) Director of Idarah Ulum Athariyah Faisalabad.
b) Khateeb Masjid Mubarak Faisalabad.
c) Member of the Majlis Idarat of the magazine *Al-Itisam.*
d) Nazim Majlis Ifta of Markazi Jamiyat Ahl e Hadith Pakistan.
e) Member of the Majlis Fuqaha Shar'iyah America (AMJA: Association of the Muslim Jurists of America).
f) Member of Majlis Idarat Al-Haramayn Jhelum.
g) Nazim e Tab' wa Talif Markazi Jami'yat Ahl e Hadith Pakistan.

Source: Adapted from *Gulistan Hadith* of Shaykh Muhammad Ishaq Bhatti and other sources.

INTRODUCTION

We praise Allah and send Salah upon His noble Messenger and upon his household and Companions and those who follow them to the day of resurrection. As for what proceeds:

The noble companions, may Allah be pleased with them, are such a blessed and respected group that Allah chose them as a link between the Messenger of Allah ﷺ and his whole community, and without them neither the Qur'an could have reached us nor its explanation that we call Sunnah and Hadith. Allah ﷻ honoured them with the titles of "best of communities (*Khayr Ummah*)" and "community following the middle path (*Ummah Wasat*)". The Prophet ﷺ gave them the duty and responsibility to "Transmit from me even if was one Ayah" and Ayah means a verse of the Quran, and it also refers to Hadith and the Sunnah of the Prophet ﷺ, even if was to be a short sentence. And this is also from his miracles, which is a clear evidence and proof of his Prophethood. Moreover, during the final pilgrimage he ﷺ said addressing a large crowd: "The present should transmit this to the absent". As a result the noble companions transmitted all his teachings to the whole world and they fulfilled the responsibility given to them by the Messenger of Allah ﷺ in the best and complete manner.

You find that the enemies of the religion have also taken the Companions as targets of their criticism, they have tried to disrepute them and used every trick to portray their blessed behaviour as treachery so the link between the community and the Prophet ﷺ becomes weak and without any great efforts they can bury the religious asset of Islam under the ground. These enemies of the religion cannot openly express their hidden animosity and hatred towards the Prophet ﷺ and their hidden feelings of spite in their hearts, so they resort to targeting the Companions. Indeed Allamah Suyuti quoted from Allamah Ad-Dinori that some heretics gathered and they decided to revile the Prophet ﷺ of the Muslims but one of their elders said that if they do such then they will be killed, so they decided to revile his noble companions and mention their defects. As it is said that "if you want to bring harm to your neighbour then kill his dog". These are the people who said that aside from Ali ؓ, all the companions are going to hell and it has also been said that Ali ؓ was a Prophet and Jibril ﷺ erred when he brought down the revelation (*Miftah Al-Jannah*: p127); may Allah protect us!

The governor of Madeenah Abdullah ibn Mus'ab said that the Caliph Mahdi asked him his position regarding the person who reviles the noble Companions and he replied that such a person was a heretic as he could not dare to revile the Prophet ﷺ so he started to revile the noble Companions, so he would thereby imply that Muhammad ﷺ accompanied evil people (*Ta'jeel Al-Man'fa'ah*: p235). Al-Khateeb Al-Baghdadi also mentioned this story with more details in *Tarikh Baghdad* (10/175).

From these details the backgrounds of those who hate the Companions and those who degrade them become clear, but the enemies of Islam despite all their stratagems could not be successful in this and they could not darken the characters of those appointed by Allah as intermediaries of integrity and truthfulness. Indeed the great scholars of Hadith and noble jurists said in unity: "The Companions are all truthful" and all the efforts of those opposing them became vein, and all praises belong to Allah for this.

At the beginning of Islam the progeny of Ibn Saba were heading this front against the Companions and little-by-little the innovators and people of Kalam (speculative rhetoric) took part in it and in later times, the Orientalists and their spiritual children have played a role in this. The scholars of truth have always refuted these people and exerted great efforts in the defence of the Companions, may Allah reward them with the best of rewards.

But it is extremely regrettable that some people calling themselves Ahlus Sunnah wal Jama'ah are, in some of their research, trying to degrade the Companions and, by mentioning their disputes and conflicts, they want to reduce their importance. Indeed they are trying continuously and actively to portray the efforts of the Companions as not solely for the sake of Islam but they claim that their efforts were based on personal benefit or liking and they were fighting like people desirous of the throne and kingship (may Allah protect us from such beliefs!)

In contrast to this, all of Ahlus Sunnah are in agreement on the fact that the decision on the internal matters and disputes between the Companions is not a matter of history but a matter of creed, and despite these conflicts they are honourable, truthful and a people who desired guidance for the community. This is the position of all the pious predecessors. The scholars who authored books on creed gave in them a great emphasis on this and we will have the pleasure to present their detailed statements to the readers of this book.

We have deliberately not discussed the status of the Companions, the topic of their integrity and the ruling on the one who insults them and neither have we discussed the religious position on those who acted in a criminal manner towards the Companions, otherwise the size of this book would have been greater. We only sufficed with mentioning the ruling of all the pious predecessors and Ahlus Sunnah Wal Jama'ah on the conflicts between the Companions so that the laymen can rectify their creed regarding them and refrain from discussing about these disputes as there is no benefit in repeating these stories. Indeed a naïve layman might have a bad opinion of the Companions, thus reducing his love for them, which is required from every truthful believer towards them.

Approximately 30 years ago, Dar Al-Ulum Al-Athariyah published an epistle on the topic of 'Adalah Sahabah (the integrity of the Companions) which was concise and very beneficial but it is regrettable that it is has not been available for some time. If Allah ﷻ confers His favour then it will be published again with additions. I invoke Allah ﷻ to accept the efforts of this person in the defence of the Companions and the great contributions of all those who took part in this good action and those in charge of this Idarah (institute) who helped immensely. Ameen O Lord of the Universe!

Irshad Al-Haqq Al-Athari
31.8. 2001

All praises belong to Allah, the Lord of the universe and may the Salah and peace be upon the leader of the Messengers and the seal of the Prophets and upon all of his companions and those who follow them up to the Day of Judgement. As for what proceeds;

All of Ahlus Sunnah agree that "The Sahabah are all truthful and upright", and after the noble Prophets (may the Salah and peace be upon them), the greatest status and nobility belongs to that of the companions. You will see great titles given to scholars who are not companions such as "imam of the religion", the jurist, the scholar of Hadith, the mujtahid, the "Shaykh Al-Islam", the "shaykh of the reformers", the "imam of the gnostics", the "role model of the wayfarers", the "chain of the complete people" and many other titles but all of these scholars will not be on par with any of the companions in the books.

The poet said: "When you said 100, then from 1 to 99, all have been included" and in the same manner when you say "companion of the Messenger of Allah ﷺ" meaning "companion" then there is no need to add any other rank. If all the other good qualities of scholars were to be gathered in a person, he would not reach the level of a companion. The Prophet ﷺ pointed at this, that if a person of great status does whatever great action he cannot reach the least good action of a companion. Indeed Abu Sa'eed Al-Khudri ﷺ narrated that the Prophet ﷺ said:

> Do not insult my companions, if one of you were to spend the equivalent of the mountain of Uhud in gold he would not reach the Mudd[1] spent by one of them, not even its half (*Sahih Al-Bukhari* with *Fathul Bari*: 7/21; *Muslim*: 2/310).

---

[1] Tr: The mudd was a type of measure equivalent to what could fill the cupped hands of a man of average size.

Rather Hafiz Ibn Hajar quoted from Imam Al-Barqani that one of the versions states: *"if one of you were to spend the equivalent of the mountain of Uhud everyday"* meaning if he was to spend such an amount everyday, he would not reach the Mudd or its half spent by a companion (*Fathul Bari*, 7/34). *Sahih Muslim* and other books mention the reason behind this statement, Khalid ibn Waleed ⚔ and AbdurRahman ibn Awf[2] ⚔ had an argument which resulted in Khalid ibn Waleed using inappropriate words towards AbdurRahman ibn Awf, and when this reached the Prophet ﷺ, he said not to say bad things about his companions.

What is to be noted is that the difference of levels among the companions is an accepted matter, those who became Muslim before the conquest of Makkah are not similar to those who became Muslim after. Indeed those who became Muslim before are better, and likewise the best among those who became Muslim before the conquest of Makkah are those who participated in the peace treaty of Hudaybiyah, and those better than them are those who participated in the Battle of Badr, and the 10 promised paradise are the best among those who participated in Badr and the four rightly guided caliphs are the best among them and Abu Bakr is the best among them. The evidences of this are mentioned in the books of creed and this is not the aim of our study here; our aim here is to the point to the fact that Khalid ibn Waleed ⚔, who has been named "a sword among the swords of Allah" on the holy tongue of the leader of the world ﷺ, despite all his services, he could not reach the level of AbdurRahman ibn Awf ⚔ and the Prophet ﷺ cautioned him against using harsh words against AbdurRahman ibn Awf, so what about a non-companion insulting or saying bad things

---

[2] AbdurRahman ibn Awf ⚔ was among the 10 Companions promised paradise. Once, due to a severe injury, he fainted. His family thought that he had passed away, and a little later he woke up and said "Allahu Akbar". His household, astonished, also said "Allahu Akbar" and he asked them: "Did I faint?" and they replied: "Yes". He said that during the state of unconsciousness two individuals came to him and said: "Come with us so we can take Allah's ruling upon you" so we went and on the way a man came and inquired: "Where are you taking him?" and the two individuals said: "We are taking him to seek Allah's judgement on him" and so he said to them: "Go back, he is among those upon whom Allah has written happiness and forgiveness while they were in the wombs of their mothers" (*Hakim*:3/307; *Al-Ma'rifah wa Tarikh*: 1/367; *As-Siyar*: 1/89, and its Isnad is authentic).

against a companion? And how can such a person reach the level of a companion? Abdullah ibn 'Umar ﷺ said:

> Do not insult the companions of Muhammad ﷺ, the standing of one of them - meaning with the Prophet ﷺ - for one hour is better that the actions of one of you during his whole life[3] (*Ibn Majah*; *Fadhail Sahabah* of Ahmad: 1/67; *As-Sunnah* of Ibn Abi Asim: 2/484; *Usul Ahlus Sunnah*: 7/1249).

Allamah Ali Qari quoted the same speech from Ibn Abbas in his *Sharh Fiqh Al-Akbar* (p68). And in the same manner Sa'eed ibn Zayd ibn Amr ibn Nufayl said:

> The participation of one among them (i.e. the companions) in a battle with the Messenger of Allah ﷺ in which his face became dusted is better that the actions of one of you during his whole life even if you were to reach the age of Nuh ﷺ. (*Abu Dawud*: 4/344; *Nasai*, and others).

NOT TOLERATING ANYTHING UNPLEASANT BEING SAID ABOUT THE COMPANIONS

Hearing anyone saying unpleasant things about his companions was unpalatable for the Prophet ﷺ. It is narrated from Abdullah ibn Masood ﷺ that he said:

> None of you should come and transmit to me something about any of my companions, for verily I like to come to you with a clean heart. (*Tirmizi* with *Tuhfah*: 4/367; *Abu Dawud* with *Al-Awn*: 4/415; *Ahmad*: 1/396, and others).

THE PROHIBITION OF INSULTING THE COMPANIONS

And likewise it is narrated from Abdullah ibn Mughafal ﷺ that the Messenger of Allah ﷺ said:

> Fear Allah. Fear Allah about my companions. Do not take them after me as targets of your criticism. Verily whoever loves them it is because of his love for me, and whoever hates them it is because of his hatred towards

---

[3] More statement of the pious predecessors regarding this will be mentioned ahead.

me, and whoever harms them he has harmed me. (*Tirmizi*: 4/360, and he declared it Hasan; Ibn Hibban declared it authentic)

Though there is critism of the two previous narrations, many authentic narrations which forbid insulting the companions support them, and the topic of all of them is the same. Indeed it is reported from Anas ﷺ that the Prophet ﷺ said: "Overlook and pardon my companions. Do not revile my companions" (*Al-Bazar*). Allamah Haythami said that the narrators of this Hadith are narrators from *Sahih Al-Bukhari* and *Muslim* (*Rijaluhu Rijaal As-Sahih*, see *Majma' Az-Zawaid*: 10/21).

And similarly it is narrated from Aishah ﷺ that the Prophet ﷺ said: "Do not insult my companions, Allah has cursed those who insult my companions" (Tabarani in *Awsat*). Allamah Haythami said that outside Ali ibn Sahl, all other narrators are narrators from *Sahih Al-Bukhari* and Ali ibn Sahl is also Thiqah (trustworthy, reliable, see *Majma' Az-Zawaid*: 10/210)

Abdullah ibn Abbas narrated from the Prophet ﷺ: "Whoever insults my companions, may the curse of Allah, the angels and all people be upon him!" (*Tabarani* in *Sahih Al-Jami*: 6285; *As-Silsilah As-Sahihah*: 2340).

Umar Al-Farooq ﷺ reported that the Prophet ﷺ said: "Look after my companions because of me" (*Ibn Majah,* p172; *Ahmad*: 1/26; *Abu Ya'la*: 1/102; *As-Sahihah*: 432, 1116). Some versions read: "Be good towards my companions".

Likewise Abdullah ibn Masood ﷺ reported from the Messenger of Allah ﷺ that he said:

> When my companions are mentioned, remain quiet. When the stars are mentioned, remain quiet, and when destiny is mentioned, remain quiet" (*Tabarani* and others; *As-Sahihah*: 34).

Muslims have faith in destiny but it is prohibited to argue and inspect it. It is forbidden as well to discuss and analyse the rulings of stars and their effects, and likewise discussing and repeating the disputes and conflicts between the Companions and raise blame and objections on them is also prohibited. Ibn Abbas ﷺ said in a Mawqoof way[4]:

---

[4] Tr: Meaning a statement attributed to a companion, i.e. Ibn Abbas' statement in this case.

O servant, beware of reviling the companions of Muhammad ﷺ as reviling them will bring poverty, and discussing and analysing the stars constitutes astrology, and denying the destiny is calling towards heresy.

Meaning: reviling the companions amounts to cancelling his actions and bringing poverty and sadness in the hereafter, may Allah protect us from such! The mother of the believers Aishah ﵂ said: "They were instructed to seek forgiveness for the companions of the Prophet ﷺ but instead they started to insult them (*Muslim*: 2/421).

The Lord of majesty and bounty, when mentioning the wealth of *Fay'* (booty obtained without fighting) or Ghanimah (booty obtained through fighting) clarified that the Muhajir and the Ansar have a right in it and also the people who came after them and seek forgiveness for them, He said:

$$وَٱلَّذِينَ جَآءُو مِنۢ بَعْدِهِمْ يَقُولُونَ رَبَّنَا ٱغْفِرْ لَنَا وَلِإِخْوَٰنِنَا ٱلَّذِينَ سَبَقُونَا بِٱلْإِيمَٰنِ وَلَا تَجْعَلْ فِى قُلُوبِنَا غِلًّا لِّلَّذِينَ ءَامَنُوا۟ رَبَّنَآ إِنَّكَ رَءُوفٌ رَّحِيمٌ$$

And [there is a share for] those who came after them, saying, "Our Lord, forgive us and our brothers who preceded us in faith and put not in our hearts [any] resentment toward those who have believed. Our Lord, indeed You are Kind and Merciful." (Al-Hashr: 10)

This is the verse towards which the mother of the believers Aishah ﵂ pointed to by saying that they were instructed to seek forgiveness for the companions but instead they started to insult them. Rather 'Abdullah ibn 'Abbas ﵁ said:

Do not revile the companions of Muhammad ﷺ as verily Allah (Azza wa Jalla) ordered us to seek forgiveness for them and He knew they would be involved in mutual fights (*Fadhail As-Sahabah* of Ahmad: 1/70 and 2/1152; *Usul I'tiqad*: 7/1245, 1250; *Ash-Sharee'ah* of Al-Aajuri: 5/2492; *Minhaj As-Sunnah*: 1/154; *As-Sarim Al-Maslul*, p574 and others).

It is narrated from Zayn Al-Abidin ﵁ that a group came to him from Iraq and they were using unsuitable speech regarding Abu Bakr, Umar and Uthman ﵁ so he said to them: "Are you from the Muhajirs?" and they replied no, and he asked them after: "Are you from the Ansar?" and they replied no, so Zayn Al-Abidin ﵁ said:

When you are not among these two categories then I attest that you are absolutely not among those about whom Allah (Ta'ala) said:

وَٱلَّذِينَ جَآءُو مِنۢ بَعْدِهِمْ يَقُولُونَ رَبَّنَا ٱغْفِرْ لَنَا وَلِإِخْوَٰنِنَا ٱلَّذِينَ سَبَقُونَا بِٱلْإِيمَٰنِ وَلَا تَجْعَلْ فِى قُلُوبِنَا غِلًّا لِّلَّذِينَ ءَامَنُوا۟ رَبَّنَآ إِنَّكَ رَءُوفٌ رَّحِيمٌ

And [there is a share for] those who came after them, saying, "Our Lord, forgive us and our brothers who preceded us in faith and put not in our hearts [any] resentment toward those who have believed," so leave this place, Allah will deal with you as you deserve.

This event has been narrated in *Hiliyah Al-Awliya* (3/137); *Tafsir Al-Qurtubi* (18/31), and with this it is also mentioned by the famous Shi'a historian Allamah Ali ibn Isa Irbili in his book *Kashf Al-Ghummah fi Ma'rifah Al-Aimah* (2/267), with the Persian translation of *Al-Manaqib*.

With all these Ahadith and narrations it is clear like the clarity in the middle of the day that Allah ﷻ has commanded us to seek forgiveness for the noble companions, and the Prophet ﷺ forbade using any bad language, putting any blame on them, insulting or reviling them, and he declared the one who does such as a person deserving to be cursed.

THE ORDER TO BE TOLERANT WITH THE COMPANIONS

It is narrated in *Sahih Al-Bukhari* and *Muslim* from Anas ibn Malik ﷺ that the Messenger of Allah ﷺ said about the noble companions from the Ansar: "Accept the good of the good-doers amongst them and excuse the wrongdoers amongst them" (*Al-Bukhari* with *Al-Fath*: 7/121; *Muslim*). This Hadith means: acknowledge their good actions and qualities and overlook their mistakes and slips. *Sahih Al-Bukhari* contains the detail that it was during the final illness of the Prophet ﷺ and a group of the Ansar were weeping while remembering the Prophet ﷺ, and Abu Bakr and Abbas ﷺ, who were passing nearby saw their state and went to see the Prophet ﷺ and mentioned to him their crying, so he came out, tying his head with a piece of the hem of a sheet due to pain in the head; he ascended the Minbar (pulpit) which he never ascended after this day. After praising Allah, he ﷺ said:

> I request you to take care of the Ansar as they are my near companions to whom I confided my private secrets. They have fulfilled their obligations and rights which were enjoined on them but there remains what is for them. So, accept the good of the good-doers amongst them and excuse the wrongdoers amongst them.

It is narrated from Abu Darda ﷺ that Abu Bakr and Umar ﷺ had an argument and Abu Bakr had apologised but Umar but he showed lack of respect and when the Prophet ﷺ was informed, he said: "Will you not leave my companion because of me" (*Bukhari* with *Al-Fath*: 7/18).

The dispute of Khalid ibn Waleed and AbdurRahman ibn Awf ﷺ has been quoted previously; regarding this event the wording of *Musnad Ahmad* and *Bazar* is: "Leave my companions because of me" (*Majma' Az-Zawaid*: 10/15).

Also consider that some of the noble companions who received good news committed some errors, but what was the consequence? At the conquest of Makkah, Hatib ibn Abi Balta'ah wrote a letter to the people of Makkah warning them that the Prophet ﷺ was about to take action against them and the details of this are present in books of Hadith and history. The summary is that this letter was caught and from the military point of view this action of Hatib ﷺ fell under rebellion against the Islamic community and this was probably the reason why Umar Farooq ﷺ said: "O Messenger of Allah, give me the permission to cut the head of this hypocrite", but the Prophet ﷺ replied that Hatib was a companion who had participated to Badr, and "don't you know that Allah (ﷻ) said about the people of Badr? Do whatever you want, you will be forgiven."

Sa'd ibn Abi Waqqas ﷺ was present when some people starting to revile Ali ﷺ so Sa'd said:

> Cease reviling the companions of the Messenger of Allah ﷺ as we committed an error in the presence of the Messenger of Allah and Allah ﷻ revealed:

$$ لَّوْلَا كِتَٰبٌ مِّنَ ٱللَّهِ سَبَقَ لَمَسَّكُمْ فِيمَآ أَخَذْتُمْ عَذَابٌ عَظِيمٌ $$

> **"If not for a decree from Allah that preceded, you would have been touched for what you took by a great punishment"** and I hope that that mercy of Allah (ﷻ) is what preceded". (*Al-Matalib Al-Aaliyah*: 4/340)

Hafiz ibn Hajar wrote after this narration: "This chain of narration is authentic and this text (Matn) contains many magnificent benefits". Imam Hakim also mentioned this narration in *Al-Mustadrak* (2/229) and declared it to be upon the condition of the two Shaykhs (Al-Bukhari and Muslim) and Allamah Dhahabi agreed with him in his *Talkhis Al-Mustadrak*.

This verse from Surah Anfal, number 68, was revealed concerning the prisoners of Badr who were freed in exchange for a ransom. This decision was not liked by Allah (ﷻ) and hence came the revelation of this verse, in which the written decree about the people of Badr means a general forgiveness. In the exegesis of this verse, the views of Sa'eed ibn Jubair, 'Ata, Mujahid, Sufyan Thawri and A'mash are the same as the view of Sa'd ﷺ (see *Ibn Katheer*: 4/360). And this is the reason why Sa'd ﷺ rebuked the people who were criticising Ali ﷺ that when Allah has decreed forgiveness for them, don't spoil your actions by reviling him.

Some of the companions were punished for drinking wine, others received the Hadd (prescribed punishment) for adultery and were absolved from this crime. Despite these mistakes it is not allowed for anyone to speak against them. At the battle of Uhud when the fight became furious, the noble companions ﷺ became dispersed and some of them left the battlefield and went to Madinah Taybah and Allah revealed about them:

إِنَّ ٱلَّذِينَ تَوَلَّوۡاْ مِنكُمۡ يَوۡمَ ٱلۡتَقَى ٱلۡجَمۡعَانِ إِنَّمَا ٱسۡتَزَلَّهُمُ ٱلشَّيۡطَٰنُ بِبَعۡضِ مَا كَسَبُواْ وَلَقَدۡ عَفَا ٱللَّهُ عَنۡهُمۡۗ إِنَّ ٱللَّهَ غَفُورٌ حَلِيمٌ

Indeed, those of you who turned back on the day the two armies met, it was Satan who caused them to slip because of some [blame] they had earned. But Allah has already forgiven them. Indeed, Allah is Forgiving and Forbearing. (Aal Imran: 155)

Pay attention that Allah ﷻ has forgiven those who had committed this shortcoming but those people who have a bad opinion about the companions and in particular about Uthman ﷺ, they are not ready to forgive them despite Allah's verdict of forgiveness!

The people of Egypt used to come forward a lot against Uthman ﷺ. It is narrated in *Sahih Al-Bukhari* that an individual from Egypt asked Abdullah ibn Umar ﷺ: "Do you know that `Uthman bin `Affan fled on the day of Uhud?" Ibn `Umar said, "Yes." He said, "Do you know that he (i.e. `Uthman) was absent from the Badr (battle) and did not join it?" Ibn `Umar said, "Yes." He said, "Do you know that he failed to be present at the Ridwan Pledge of allegiance (i.e. Pledge of allegiance at Hudaibiya) and did not witness it?" Ibn `Umar replied, "Yes". He then said, "Allahu- Akbar!" (Implying how can he be a caliph with these mistakes?) Ibn `Umar said,

> Come along; I will inform you and explain to you about what you have asked. As for the flight (of `Uthman) on the day of Uhud, I testify that Allah forgave him. As regards his absence from the Badr (battle), he was married to the daughter of Allah's Messenger (ﷺ) and she was ill, so the Prophet (ﷺ) said to him, "You will have such a reward as a man who has

fought the Badr battle will get, and will also have the same share of the booty." As for his absence from the Ridwan pledge of allegiance if there had been anybody more respected by the Meccans than 'Uthman bin 'Affan, the Prophet would surely have sent that man instead of 'Uthman. So the Prophet (ﷺ) sent him (i.e. 'Uthman to Mecca) and the Ridwan pledge of allegiance took place after 'Uthman had gone to Mecca. The Prophet raised his right hand saying. "This is the hand of 'Uthman," and clapped it over his other hand and said, "This is for 'Uthman."

Ibn 'Umar then said (to the man), "Go now, after taking this information." (*Bukhari*: 1/523). The statement of ibn Umar (ﷺ) that Allah (ﷺ) forgave him is based on the verse that we have mentioned previously:

$$إِنَّ ٱلَّذِينَ تَوَلَّوْاْ مِنكُمْ يَوْمَ ٱلْتَقَى ٱلْجَمْعَانِ إِنَّمَا ٱسْتَزَلَّهُمُ ٱلشَّيْطَنُ بِبَعْضِ مَا كَسَبُواْ وَلَقَدْ عَفَا ٱللَّهُ عَنْهُمْ إِنَّ ٱللَّهَ غَفُورٌ حَلِيمٌ$$

Indeed, those of you who turned back on the day the two armies met, it was Satan who caused them to slip because of some [blame] they had earned. But Allah has already forgiven them. Indeed, Allah is Forgiving and Forbearing. (Aal Imran: 155)

You can assess what kinds of stories were concocted by animosity against Uthman (ﷺ) and these stories are totally contrary to the truth, entirely baseless and part of a propaganda campaign[5].

---

[5] Hasan Al-Basri said: "The leader of the believers Uthman ibn Affan (ﷺ) acted for 12 years and none objected anything from his rule until the Fasaqah (corrupt people) appreaed" (*At-Tarikh As-Sagheer* of Al-Bukhari, p24). And when some people raised objections to some of his dealings then Ali (ﷺ) came to his defence. In the recent past one of the greatest critics of Uthman (ﷺ) could not but acknowledge this reality: "The people who made a front were not representing any area rather they established a conspiring party. When they came outside Madeenah, they tried to make Ali, Talha and Zubayr (ﷺ) join them but these three rebuffed them. Ali (ﷺ) replied to each of their claims and cleared the position of Uthman (ﷺ). The Muhajirun and Ansar of Madeenah, who had the status of Ahlul Aqd of the actual Islamic state, were not inclined to join them but they [the rebels] remained firm on their stubbornness" (see *Khilafat wa Mulukiyat*).

We do not want to give length to this topic, this is not our subject, but we cannot abstain from mentioning that the Prophet (ﷺ) declared Uthman (ﷺ) to be a martyr and the narrations on this topic reach the level of Tawatur. If the claims of the objectors were correct, what is the meaning of the martyrdom of Uthman (ﷺ) and the support of his position? Murrah

Allah ﷻ is the knower of the unseen and knows the position of everyone. He knows the qualities and shortcomings of the companions ﷺ. He affirmed openly His satisfaction of them:

وَٱلسَّٰبِقُونَ ٱلْأَوَّلُونَ مِنَ ٱلْمُهَٰجِرِينَ وَٱلْأَنصَارِ وَٱلَّذِينَ ٱتَّبَعُوهُم بِإِحْسَٰنٍ رَّضِىَ ٱللَّهُ عَنْهُمْ وَرَضُوا۟ عَنْهُ وَأَعَدَّ لَهُمْ جَنَّٰتٍ تَجْرِى تَحْتَهَا ٱلْأَنْهَٰرُ خَٰلِدِينَ فِيهَآ أَبَدًا ذَٰلِكَ ٱلْفَوْزُ ٱلْعَظِيمُ

And the first forerunners [in the faith] among the Muhajireen and the Ansar and those who followed them with good conduct - Allah is pleased with them and they are pleased with Him, and He has prepared for them gardens beneath which rivers flow, wherein they will abide forever. That is the great attainment. (At-Tawbah: 100)

ibn Ka'b ﷺ narrates that he heard the Messenger of Allah ﷺ mentioning turmoils. A man walked with a piece of cloth on his head and he ﷺ said: "This one will be upon guidance on this day", so I stood to look who this person was and it was Uthman ibn Affan. I made the face of Uthman turn towards the Prophet ﷺ and I asked him: "Did you say this about him?" and he replied: "Yes". This narration is in *Jami Tirmizi* with *At-Tuhfah* (4/322), *Ibn Majah* (p11) and *Musnad Ahmad* (4/236). Imam Tirmizi declared it to be Hasan Sahih (*Mishkat*, 3/1715) and it is also mentioned in *Sahih Sunnan Tirmizi*. Also see *Kitab As-Sunnah* (2/591), *Al-Ahadith wal Mathani* of Ibn Ibn Abi Asim, Tabarani in *Kabeer* (20/316) and others. Rather the same narration is narrated with approximately the same words by Ka'b ibn Hujrah with an authentic chain of narration, which has been collected by Imam ibn Majah, Ibn Abi Asim and others.

Hence when the Prophet ﷺ with his tongue of revelation supported the position of Uthman ﷺ at the times of turmoils and declared it to be truth and guidance, then what is opening one's mouth now and launching a campaign of revilement and insinuations against him except ruining one's hereafter? Not only this, in *Sahih ibn Hibban* (*Al-Mawarid*, p539, *Al-Ihsan*, 9/31) *Tabarani* (20/316) and *As-Sunnah li Ibn Abi 'Asim* (2/591) it is narrated with an authentic narration from Murrah ibn Ka'b ﷺ, which Allamah Albani mentioned in *Sahih Mawarid Az-Zaman* (2/347) and *Silsilah As-Saheehah*, n.3118, that: we were going with the Prophet ﷺ towards Madinah and he said: "What will you do at the time when the turmoil will be spread on the earth like the horns of a cow?" We asked him: "O Prophet of Allah, what shall we do at this time?" He ﷺ replied: "Attach yourself to this man and his companions". The wording of Tabarani is: "Follow this man and his companions". Murrah ﷺ said that he looked at this man and it was Uthman ﷺ. I held him and turned his face towards the Prophet ﷺ and I asked him: "O Messenger of Allah, is this the person about whom you said such?" and he replied: "Yes, it is about him". So not only did he affirm the truthfulness of Uthman ﷺ but he also ordered to be with him and follow him. Now this is a matter of religion and faith for every Muslim, he considers Uthman to be upon the truth and he condemns those who took steps against him.

After mentioning the different levels among the companions, Allah ﷻ has clearly promised good for all of them, not for a group among them. He said:

لَا يَسْتَوِى مِنكُم مَّنْ أَنفَقَ مِن قَبْلِ ٱلْفَتْحِ وَقَٰتَلَ أُوْلَٰٓئِكَ أَعْظَمُ دَرَجَةً مِّنَ ٱلَّذِينَ أَنفَقُواْ مِنۢ بَعْدُ وَقَٰتَلُواْ وَكُلًّا وَعَدَ ٱللَّهُ ٱلْحُسْنَىٰ وَٱللَّهُ بِمَا تَعْمَلُونَ خَبِيرٌ

Not equal among you are those who spent before the conquest [of Makkah] and fought [and those who did so after it]. Those are greater in degree than they who spent afterwards and fought. But to all Allah has promised the best [reward]. And Allah, with what you do, is acquainted. (Al-Hadid: 10)

Likewise Allah ﷻ said:

إِنَّ ٱلَّذِينَ سَبَقَتْ لَهُم مِّنَّا ٱلْحُسْنَىٰٓ أُوْلَٰٓئِكَ عَنْهَا مُبْعَدُونَ

Indeed, those for whom the best [reward] has preceded from Us - they are from it far removed. (Al-Anbiya: 101)

Hafiz Ibn Hazm took evidences from these verses that all companions are definitively from the people of paradise (*Al-Isabah*: 1/7). This was also affirmed by Imam Bayhaqi in *Al-I'tiqad wal Hidayah ila Sabeel Ar-Rashad ala Mazhab As-Salaf wa Ashabil Hadith* that all the companions are forgiven and from the people of paradise. We cannot say definitely that all the companions are infallible and cannot sin, but it is a reality that they are, compared to the community, more honest, more truthful in their speech and upright, and if they committed errors or sins then in comparison they will have good actions which will expiate their sins and the scale of their good actions will outweigh their shortcomings in all cases. And this is why Allah ﷻ expressed His satisfaction with them in many places and He praised their faith and sincerity; He declared them as a criterion for faith; He declared those who doubt their faith as hypocrites and those who revile them as despicable people; He gave them the good news of success and triumph in this world and in the hereafer and also said:

وَلَٰكِنَّ ٱللَّهَ حَبَّبَ إِلَيْكُمُ ٱلْإِيمَٰنَ وَزَيَّنَهُۥ فِى قُلُوبِكُمْ وَكَرَّهَ إِلَيْكُمُ ٱلْكُفْرَ وَٱلْفُسُوقَ وَٱلْعِصْيَانَ أُوْلَٰٓئِكَ هُمُ ٱلرَّٰشِدُونَ

But Allah has endeared to you the faith and has made it pleasing in your hearts and has made hateful to you disbelief, defiance and disobedience. Those are the [rightly] guided. (Al-Hujurat: 7)

By announcing that faith has settled in their heart, Allah (ﷻ) made them hate disbelief, corruption and disobedience. Pay attention to the fact that the context and reason for revelation of this verse is about Waleed ibn 'Uqbah ؓ, who was sent by the Messenger of Allah ﷺ to collect Zakah from Banu Mustaliq; this matter is established according to historians that Waleed ؓ became Muslim at the conquest of Makkah, so this occurred after the conquest of Makkah, and the people who were honoured with companionship (of the Prophet ﷺ) at this time, the Lord of the great throne said that disbelief, defiance and disobedience have been made hateful in their hearts. Hafiz Ibn Katheer said that "Fusuq" means a major sin and "'Isiyan" means all kinds of sins (*Tafsir ibn Katheer*: 4/268), meaning that all the companions hated all major and minor sins; Allah (ﷻ) had created this hatred in their hearts. Therefore, after this clear announcement, thinking that they made mistakes purposely and deliberately just for worldly gains, is synonymous to ruining one's hereafter. Without any doubt some errors occurred from some companions due to circumstances and some occurred as well during the era of the Prophet ﷺ, and the consequence of their sins can be seen through their worries and regret as mentioned in Ahadith in the books of Hudud. The Prophet ﷺ, by applying the ruling of Allah, purified them and proclaimed that if their repentance was shared among 70 sinners of Madeenah, it would be enough for all of them. And we have to understand some events that occurred after his death ﷺ in the same manner.

After this necessary clarification, this matter has become apparent that Allah ﷻ, by announcing their general forgiveness, has declared them to be from the people of paradise. The Prophet ﷺ insisted on overlooking over their mistakes and he said to forgive them because of him, and now it is a matter for the religion and faith of each person to overlook mistakes of the noble companions because of them being companions of the Messenger ﷺ and not to mention them publically on pulpits and the Mihrab so that they become objects of ridicule.

Moreover the Prophet ﷺ forbade declaring the companions as evil and using inappropriate words about them, rather he declared those who launch campaigns of insults and revilements against them as cursed people, and he invoked the curse of Allah, His angels and His servants upon them. And this is why the scholars of this community declared the perpetrators of such actions as people committing major sins, and they declared attacking the honour of the companions, mentioning their defects, reviling and mocking them as Haram (forbidden).

Some people want to relax the veins of their hearts by giving air to exaggerations in the conflicts, differences and disputes that occurred between the noble companions. The result of their impure action is that some people will have a bad opinion about the companions in general and about Uthman, Mu'awiyah and 'Amr ibn 'Aas ﷺ in particular. Such people won't mention their names with respect; rather they will make fun of those who defend them.

We want to establish here with the statements of the scholars of the Salaf that it is not correct to make the conflicts among the companions and their internal differences as a matter of discussion, rather the books containing the creed of Ahlus Sunnah warned against this. Indeed this issue is not an ordinary issue but an issue concerning the creed of the people of Islam that one should remain silent on the conflicts of the companions.

THE STATEMENT OF 'UMAR IBN ABDIL AZEEZ

The rightly guided caliph 'Umar ibn Abdil Azeez was asked about those who participated in the battle of Siffin, so he replied: "Allah has preserved us from this blood so I prefer not to taint my tongue with it" (*Al-Hiliyah*: 9/114, 129; *Jami' Bayan Al-'Ilm*: 2/93; *Adaab Ash-Shafi'i*: 314; *Manaqib Ash-Shafi'i*: 1/449; *Ibn Sa'd*: 5/382).

Imam Abu Bakr Ahmad ibn Muhammad Al-Khallal also quoted from him that when he was asked about the battles of Siffin and Jamal, then he replied: "A matter from which Allah took my hands away, I will not enter my tongue in it" (*As-Sunnah* of Al-Khallal, p462).

Despite his uprightness, Umar ibn Abdil Azeez would not tolerate to hear anything against Mu'awiyah ﷺ. Ibrahim ibn Maysarah said that he saw Umar (ibn Abdil Azeez) whipping a person, as this person had reviled Mu'awiyah ﷺ, and he was thus punished by flogging (*Al-Bidayah*: 8/139; Ibn Sa'd: 5/384, and others).

THE STATEMENT OF IMAM SHAFI'I

The previous statement of Umar ibn Abdil Azeez has also been mentioned by Imam Shafi'i. Indeed Allamah Ali Qari quoted from Imam Shafi'i that he said:

"Allah has preserved our hands from this blood so I prefer not to involve my tongue in it" (*Sharh Fiqh Al-Akbar*, p71).

He also said to his student Rabee': "O Rabee' do not embark upon discussing about the companions of the Messenger of Allah ﷺ as verily tomorrow your opponent will be the Prophet ﷺ" (*Siyar A'lam An-Nubala*: 10/28).

He also said: "I don't see the people who are tested with insulting the companions of the Messenger of Allah ﷺ except that by this Allah increases them (ie companions) in reward after the cessation of their actions" (*Manaqib Shafi'i*: 1/441; *Usul Al-I'tiqad*: 8/1460).

A similar statement is reported from 'A'ishah ﵂ that when she was asked about people reviling the companions and even Abu Bakr and Umar ﵂, she said: "What is strange with this? Their actions ceased so Allah loved that their reward would not be cut" (*Jam' Al-Fawaid*: 2/249; *Jami Al-Usul*[6]: 8/554).

THE STATEMENT OF IMAM AHMAD IBN HANBAL

Imam Abu Bakr Al-Marwazi said that Imam Ahmad was asked about his opinion about Ali and Mu'awiyah ﵂ and he replied: "I do not say about them except good, may Allah have mercy on all of them" (*As-Sunnah* of Al-Khallal, p460; *Manaqib Ahmad*, p164).

Allamah ibn Al-Jawzi also quoted from Imam Abu Bakr Al-Marwazi that Imam Ahmad mentioned the noble companions and he said:

> May Allah have mercy on all of them, on Mu'awiyah, 'Amr ibn Al-'Aas, Abu Musa, Al-Mughirah ﵂; Allah (Ta'ala) described all of them in His Book and said:

$$\text{سِيمَاهُمْ فِي وُجُوهِهِم مِّنْ أَثَرِ ٱلسُّجُودِ}$$

> **"Their mark is on their faces from the trace of prostration"** (*Manaqib Ahmad*, p164; *As-Sunnah* of Al-Khallal, p477).

---

[6] Hafiz Ibn Taymiyah in *Minhaj As-Sunnah* (1/153) and Allamah ibn Abil 'Izz in his *Sharh Aqidah Tahawiyah* (p530) attributed it to *Sahih Muslim*, but despite researching I could not find this narration in it, Allah ﷻ knows best.

Rather Allamah Dhahabi mentioned that he would not like to explain in detail and repeat the famous Hadith about Ammar ibn Yasir ﷺ: "The rebellious group will kill him". He said: "He would dislike to discus about it more than this" (*As-Siyar*: 1/421). Whatever has been said in discussing and repeating this Hadith and its extrapolation, this matter is not hidden for those interested by this topic and it is not the subject of our discussion; you can measure by the feelings of Imam Ahmad that he would feel that it is inappropriate at all to dwell into these issues.

AbdulMalik ibn AbdulHameed Al-Maymuni said that he asked Imam Ahmad: "Did the Prophet ﷺ not say: "Every links established due to marriage (father-in-law, brother-in-law, son-in-law, etc.) and lineage will be cut except my links established through marriage and lineage (on the day of resurrection)" So he replied: "Yes this is the statement of the Messenger of Allah ﷺ". So I inquired: "Will this link benefit Mu'awiyah?" and he replied: "Yes he has this honour" (*As-Sunnah* of Al-Khallal, p432).

This is the reason why when Ahmad ibn Humayd Abu Talib asked Imam Ahmad whether Mu'awiyah and 'Abdullah ibn Umar were maternal uncles of the believers, as the daughter of Abu Sufiyan ﷺ, Umm Habeebah ﵂ was the wife of the Messenger of Allah ﷺ and the mother of the believers and the sister of Mu'awiyah ﷺ, and likewise Hafsah ﵂, the wife of the Prophet ﷺ, was the sister of Abdullah ibn Umar ﷺ, then Imam Ahmad replied: "Mu'awiyah and Abdullah ibn Umar are maternal uncles of the believers" (*As-Sunnah* of Al-Khallal, p433).

The aim of it in reality is to express their closeness and link to the Prophet ﷺ due to the sanctity and respect towards the pure wives of the Prophet ﷺ who are the mothers of the believers as Allah (Ta'ala) said in his noble speech:

$$\text{وَأَزْوَٰجُهُۥٓ أُمَّهَٰتُهُمْ}$$

His wives are their mothers (Al-Ahzab 33: 6)...

But by being mothers, all the links of lineage are not established for them, and this is why it is allowed (for the believers) to marry their sisters. For the details of this refer to *Minhaj As-Sunnah*: 2/199).

The idea of Mu'awiyah ﷺ being the maternal uncle of the believers was present in his era. Indeed Hafiz Ibn Katheer wrote that the prisoners of the battle of Siffin were freed by Ali ﷺ on his return from there. Mu'awiyah ﷺ also had prisoners and he thought first that 'Ali had killed the prisoners from his group, so he wanted to kill his prisoners but when he came to know that 'Ali had freed his prisoners, Mu'awiyah also freed his prisoners. Among these prisoners was 'Amr ibn Aws Azdi. At the time Mu'awiyah wanted to kill him, he said: "O my maternal uncle! Show pity on me!" Mu'awiyah asked: "How am I your maternal uncle?" He replied: "The mother of the believers Umm Habeebah is the wife of the Prophet ﷺ and for this reason she is the mother of the believers, I am her son and you are her brother and my maternal uncle." Mu'awiyah ﷺ was amazed by such and left him (*Al-Bidayah*: 7/278).

Qadhi Abu Ya'la wrote an epistle in defence of Ameer Mu'awiyah which is entitled: *Tanzih Khal Al-Muminin Mu'awiyah ibn Abi Sufiyan min Zulm wal Fisq fi Mutalabah Bi Damm Ameer Al-Muminin Uthman radhi Allah Anhuma* (Purification of the maternal uncle of the believers Mu'awiyah ibn Abi Sufiyan from injustice and corruption in seeking the retaliation for the blood of the leader of the believers Uthman, may Allah be pleased with both of them). Pay attention to the fact that he named Mu'awiyah as the maternal uncle of the believers in the title of the book. 'Umar ibn 'Ali ibn Samurah Al-Jam'adi wrote when mentioning Mu'awiyah ﷺ: "Then the maternal uncle of the believers and the scribe of the revelation of the Lord of the universe became the leader" (*Tabaqat Fuqaha Al-Yaman*, p47).

It is narrated with an authentic chain that Imam Ahmad was asked about an individual who says that he doesn't consider Mua'wiyah ﷺ as the scribe of the revelation and neither as the maternal uncle of the believers, and he replied:

> This statement is rejected and evil, people should stay far away from him and should not sit next to him. We warn people from such individuals. (*As-Sunnah* of Al-Khallal, p434)

Imam Ahmad was also asked whether Mu'awiyah ﷺ was superior or 'Umar ibn Abdil 'Azeez, so he replied: "Mu'awiyah is superior, we do not compare anyone to the companions of the Messenger of Allah ﷺ" (*As-Sunnah* of Al-Khallal, pp435, 434 and 477). Rather Imam Ahmad would say whenever he would see someone reviling or mentioning in a disrespectful manner a companion that his Islam is doubtful; his words are: "If you see anyone mentioning the companions of the Messenger of Allah ﷺ in a bad manner, suspect his Islam" (*Usul I'tiqad*: 7/1252; *As-Sarim Al-Maslul*).

Likewise he was informed about a person who considers Umar ibn Abdil Azeez to be superior to Mu'awiyah ﷺ, and he said: "Do not sit with him, do not eat with him, do not drink with him, and if he is ill do not visit him"

(*Az-Zayl ala Tabaqat Al-Hanabilah* of Ibn Rajab; 1/133). Rather he would instruct not to pray behind someone who would say bad things about Mu'awiyah ﷺ (*Al-Manhaj li Ahmad*; 1/255). From these statements we can estimate the position of Imam Ahmad regarding this issue.

THE STATEMENT OF IMAM MU'AFA IBN 'IMRAN

Imam Mu'afa ibn Imran (d. 184 AH) is a famous jurist, Muhadith and pious worshiper from Mosul. He was a student of Imam Sufiyan Thawri, Imam Awza'i, Imam ibn Jurayj, Imam Hammad ibn Salamah and others and among the teachers of Abdullah ibn Mubarak, Imam Wakee' and others. He had the title of "Yaqut Al-Ulama" and he is a narrator of *Sahih Al-Bukhari*.

Someone asked him what is the difference between 'Umar ibn Abdil Azeez and Mu'awiyah ﷺ, and the narrator said:

> I saw him becoming extremely angry and he said: "No one is compared to the companions of Muhammad ﷺ, Mu'awiyah ﷺ is his scribe, his companion, his relative through marriage and his trusted one upon the revelation of Allah (ﷻ)" and he said: "The Messenger of Allah ﷺ said: 'Leave my companions and relatives through marriage because of me, and whoever insults them, may the curse of Allah, His angels and all people be upon him'. (*Ash-Shari'ah*; p2467; *Sharh Usul I'tiqad*; 8/1445; *Tarikh Baghdad*; 1/209; *Al-Bidayah*; 8/139, and others)

Bishr Hafi said that Imam Mu'afa ibn 'Imran was asked whether Mu'awiyah ﷺ is superior or Umar ibn Abdil Azeez, and he heard him replying: "Mu'awiyah ﷺ is superior to 600 Umar ibn Abdil Azeezs'" (*As-Sunnah* of Al-Khallal).

WAS MU'AWIYAH THE SCRIBE OF REVELATION?

The closeness of Mu'awiyah ﷺ to the Prophet ﷺ is not hidden to anyone, for he was the scribe of the Messenger of Allah ﷺ, rather, he was the scribe of the revelation as affirmed by Imam Mu'afi. Shaykh Al-Islam ibn Taymiyah also wrote: "He used to write the revelation so he is among those entrusted by the Prophet ﷺ in writing the revelation" (*Minhaj As-Sunnah*; 4/11). See also *Minhaj* (2/214), and note that Hafiz Ibn Hazm wrote:

> Zayd ibn Thabit ﷺ was the most devoted to writing the revelation, then Mu'awiyah ﷺ joined him after the conquest (of Makkah) so it was as if they were both devoted to writing the revelation in front of the Prophet

and other than it, and they had no other task than this" (*Jawami' As-Seerah*, p27).

Allamah Nawawi wrote: "Those who used to write the revelation the most were Zayd ibn Thabit and Mu'awiyah " (*Tahzib Al-Asma*: 1/29), and the same has been said by Allamah Ibn Al-Jawzi in *Talqih Fuhum Ahlil Asr* (p37) and *Al-Mudhish* (p43), and similar to this has been said by Qadhi 'Iyad in *Ash-Shifa* and 'Allamah Al-Khafaji in *Sharh Naseem Ar-Riyadh* (3/430); Hafiz Ibn Katheer repeated this in *Al-Bidayah* (8/21, 117, 119, 122); as did Allamah Dhahabi in *Tarikh Al-Islam* (2/309), in *Siyar* (3/123); Allamah Fasi in *Al-'Aqd Ath-Thameen* (6/910); Allamah Ibnul 'Imad in *Shazarat Az-Zahab* (1/65); 'Allamah Umar ibn Ali in Samurah in *Tabaqat Fuqaha Al-Yaman* (p47); 'Allamah Ibn Qudamah in *Lum'ah Al-I'tiqad* (p79 of the translation); 'Allamah Ibn Hajar Haytami in *Tathir Al-Jannan* (p10), the author of *Mishkat* Allamah Abu Abdillah Muhammad ibn Abdillah Al-Khateeb in *Kamal,* all of them said that he was a scribe of revelation.

Abul Hasan Ali ibn Muhammad Al-Mada'ini (d. 224 AH) said that Mu'awiyah was only a scribe for prophetic letters and some later scholars based on his statement wrote that he was not a scribe of the revelation, but rejecting the opposing statement of Imam Mu'afa ibn Imran who is more ancient and more trustworthy than Abul Hasan Al-Mada'ini is not correct. It is narrated with an authentic chain from Imam Ahmad that he was asked: "What do you say, may Allah have mercy upon you, about the one who says: "I do not say that Mu'awiyah is the scribe of revelation"?" and he replied: "This statement is evil and rejected, avoid such people and do not sit with them and warn the people about their matter" (*As-Sunnah* of Al-Khallal, p434) and this proves that Mu'awiyah being a scribe of revelation is certain and not a matter of difference. Some of the Shi'ah historians as well acknowledged this reality and most of the historians and people of knowledge said that he was a scribe of revelation; rather the conferred honour Zayd ibn Thabit had in this regard, Mu'awiyah was joined in it as affirmed by Hafiz Ibn Hazm.

THE VERDICT OF IMAM AL-'AWAM IBN HAWSHAB

Imam Al-'Awam ibn Hawshab (d. 148 AH) is counted among the Atba Tabi'in (followers of the students of the companions). He was the teachers of great scholars such as Shu'bah, Imam Yazeed ibn Harun and Haytham and is counted among the trustworthy scholars of Hadith. Shihab ibn Karash said that Imam Al-'Awam said:

> Mention the qualities of the companions of Muhammad ﷺ so they become beloved to the hearts and do not mention the conflicts between them so that people become excited against them (*As-Sunnah* of Al-Khallal, p513; *Ash-Shari'ah* of Al-Ajurri, 5/2493).

Rather Shihab ibn Kharash said:

> I reached the greatest personalities of this era and they instructed the mentioning of the qualities of the noble companions and not to mention their disputes so people become excited against them (*As-Siyar*: 8/285; *Tahzib Al-Kamal* of Al-Mizzi: 8/402, and others).

THE STATEMENT OF ABDULLAH IBN MUBARAK

The famous Muhadith, jurist, Mujahid and pious Imam Abdullah ibn Mubarak was very precautious regarding these issues. We can have a measure of his precaution from this statement: "The sword which ran among the companions was a Fitnah (trial, turmoil) and I do not say about any of them that they were Maftun (captivated in this trial)" (*As-Siyar*: 8/405). You can compare the precaution of the Salaf to the actions that are being carried on (nowadays).

Imam Abdullah ibn Mubarak was asked who was the superior between Mu'awiyah ؓ and Umar ibn Abdil 'Azeez, and he replied: "By Allah, the dust which entered the nose of the horse of Mu'awiyah ؓ with which he accompanied the Messenger of Allah ﷺ is better than 'Umar a thousand times. Mu'awiyah ؓ prayed behind the Messenger of Allah ﷺ, when the latter said: "May Allah hear the one who praises Him", Mu'awiyah replied: "Our Lord, the praise belongs to You!" What is a greater nobility than this?" (*Tathir Al-Jannan*, p10-11; *As-Sawaiq Al-Muharraqah*, p213; *Al-Bidayah*: 8/139; *Minhaj As-Sunnah*: 3/183; *Ash-Shari'ah*: 5/2466).

THE STATEMENT OF HAMMAD IBN USAMAH

Imam Hammad ibn Usamah ibn Zayd (d. 201 AH) is counted among the great scholars of Hadith; he is among the teachers of illustrious scholars such as Imam Shafi'i, Imam Ahmad, Imam Yahya, Imam Ishaq ibn Rahawayah, and Imam Ibn Abi Shaybah. Someone asked him who was superior among Mu'awiyah ؓ and Umar ibn Abdil Azeez ؓ and he replied: "No one is comparable to the companions of the Messenger of Allah ﷺ." (*Ash-Shari'ah*: 5/2465; *As-Sunnah*, p435; *Jami' Bayan Al-'Ilm*; 2/185)

The statements of the Salaf are clear regarding this, they would not equate anyone among the great Tabi'is with the companions in any way. Despite the differences among the companions, they would respect them all and would not blame any of them or revile them.

THE STATEMENT OF IMAM IBN BATTAH

Imam Abu 'Abdillah Ubaydullah ibn Muhammad ibn Battah Al-'Ukbari (d. 387 AH), explaining the view of the Salaf, wrote:

> And after this we remain silent about the conflicts that occurred between the companions of the Messenger of Allah ﷺ; they were witness of events with him and preceded people in virtue. Allah has forgiven them and has ordered you to seek forgiveness for them and obtain closeness to Him through love towards them. He made this compulsory on the tongue of His Prophet ﷺ while He knew what would happen between them and that they would fight between each other. He only favoured them upon the whole creation because they do not err on purpose and whatever conflicts occurred between them are forgiven for them and the events of Siffin, Al-Jamal and the Event of the House (of 'Uthman) and all the disputes which occurred between should not be looked into, and do not write them for yourself or for others, do not narrate then from anyone and do not read them upon other than yourselves and do not listen to those who narrate them; upon this agreed the leaders of the scholars of this community in forbidding what we have described, and among such scholars were Hammad ibn Zayd, Yunus ibn 'Ubayd, Sufiyan Ath-Thawri, Sufiyan ibn 'Uyaynah, Abdullah ibn Idris, Malik ibn Anas, Ibn Abi Zi'b, Ibn Al-Munkadir, Ibn Al-Mubarak, Shu'ayb ibn Harb, Abu Ishaq Al-Fazari, Yusuf ibn Asbat, Ahmad ibn Hanbal, Bishr ibn Al-Harith and AbdulWahab Al-Warraq, all of them narrated the forbiddance of such a matter, to scrutinise or listen to it, and they warned about delving into it and devoting oneself to it.

We can understand the position of the pious predecessors of this community from this detailed expose of Imam Ibn Battah, and this is the requirement of the authenticity of faith and its safety, and this corresponds to the high level and status of the companions, that one overlooks the differences between them and seeks forgiveness for all of them without any exception as mentioned in the verse:

رَبَّنَا ٱغْفِرْ لَنَا وَلِإِخْوَانِنَا ٱلَّذِينَ سَبَقُونَا بِٱلْإِيمَٰنِ

Our Lord forgive us and our brothers who preceded us in faith. (59:10)

The pious predecessors have carried with consistency this view in their books on creed and Sunnah, reflecting this thought and methodology within the creed of Ahlus Sunnah.

THE STATEMENTS OF IMAM AL-HASAN IBN 'ALI AL-BARBAHARI

Imam Abu Muhammad Al-Hasan ibn 'Ali ibn Khalaf Al-Barbahari (d. 329 AH) said in *Sharh As-Sunnah*:

> The best in this community after the death of the Prophet ﷺ is Abu Bakr, Umar and Uthman ﷺ. This is how it was narrated to us by Ibn Umar, he said: "We used to say while the Messenger of Allah ﷺ was among us: the best among the people after the Messenger of Allah ﷺ is Abu Bakr, Umar and 'Uthman." And the Prophet ﷺ would hear such words and not object to them. And then the best among them were 'Ali, Talhah, Az-Zubayr, Sa'd ibn Abi Waqqas, Sa'eed ibn Zayd, AbdurRahman ibn 'Awf and Abu 'Ubaydah ibn Al-Jarrah ﷺ, and all of them were suitable for the caliphate. Then the best after them are those of the first generation among which are the Muhajirun and the Ansar and they are those who prayed towards both Qiblahs (Jerusalem and then Makkah). And then the best after them are those who accompanied the Messenger of Allah ﷺ one day, one month or a year or less than this or more. Forgiveness is sought for them, their virtue is mentioned, and one remains silent about their errors, and none of them are mentioned except with good due to the statement of the Messenger of Allah ﷺ: "When my companions are mentioned, refrain (from criticising them)" and Sufyan ibn 'Uyaynah said: "Whoever speaks one word against the companions of the Messenger of Allah ﷺ, then he is among the people of desire." (*Sharh As-Sunnah*: pp74-75)

Qadhi Abul Husayn Muhammad ibn Abi Al-'Ali quoted in *Tabaqat Al-Hannabilah* from *Sharh As-Sunnah* under the mention of Imam Barbahari. Thus in *Tabaqat Al-Hannabilah* (2:21) the quote above can be seen, and there are further quotes in the same book from Imam Barbahari regarding this issue:

> Refraining (from speaking) about the wars between 'Ali, Mu'awiyah, 'A'ishah, Talhah and Az-Zubayr ﷺ and the one who was with them is not

to be argued about, and all their matters are with Allah. (*Sharh As-Sunnah*: p109; *Tabaqat Al-Hannabilah*: 2/34)

Likewise he said in *Sharh As-Sunnah* (p112; *Tabaqat*: 2/35-36 in a summarised manner) that whoever reviles the noble companions is an innovator. Do not mention the weaknesses of the companions and do not listen to anything against them as listening to such things does not keep the heart safe. Reflect on his words wherein he said:

> Know that whoever degrades any of the companions of the Messenger of Allah ﷺ, he intended to degrade the Messenger of Allah ﷺ and he harmed him in his grave. (*Sharh As-Sunnah*: p120; *Tabaqat Al-Hannabilah*: 2/37)

May Allah preserve us from such! Pointing at the straight path, he said: "Whoever puts forward the four (companions) over the rest of them and seeks mercy on the rest and seeks forgiveness for their errors, he is upon the correct path of guidance in this matter" (*Tabaqat Al-Hannabilah:* 2/41).

THE STATEMENT OF IMAM MUHAMMAD IBN AL-HUSAYN AL-AAJURRI

Imam Abu Bakr Muhammad ibn Al-Husayn ibn Abdillah Aajurri (d. 360 AH) titled a chapter in his famous book *Kitab Ash-Sharee'ah* (no. 257): "Bab Zikr Al-Kaf 'amma Shajara Bayna Ashab Rasulillah ﷺ, Rahmatullahi aleyhim Ajmaeen" (Chapter on refraining from speaking about the conflicts between the companions of the Messenger of Allah ﷺ, may the mercy of Allah be upon all of them!) Imam Aajurri discussed the subject in this chapter with great detail, bringing many evidences for his view over ten pages. Omitting the evidences he presents, we will suffice with presenting his views in a summarised manner:

> Whatever we have written regarding the virtues of the companions and Ahlul Bayt, it is necessary for the one who ponders over them to love them all, to invoke mercy for them, and to take his love for them as an intermediary towards Allah. Whatever differences occurred between them, he should not mention them, he should not search for them and discuss them. We have received the order to seek forgiveness for them and invoke mercy for them, and we have received the order to respect and follow them, as is indicated by the noble Quran, Prophetic Ahadith

and the statements of the Imams of the Muslims. There is no need for us to mention the differences between the companions, they have been honoured with the company and familial links with the Messenger of Allah ﷺ, and due to this honour Allah has announced forgiveness for them and has given them the guarantee that none of them will be ashamed on the Day of Resurrection. Allah ﷻ mentioned their qualities in the Torah and Injeel and praised them abundantly, He mentioned their repentance and His satisfaction of them. If someone says that he only intends to increase his knowledge regarding these conflicts so he can avoid the situations in which they were tested, then he is a person seeking Fitnah (turmoil) as he is pursuing a quest which can bring loss to him and there is no benefit expected from this. Instead of this, if he tries to reform himself through completing the obligatory acts and avoiding prohibited matters, this would be better for him, especially at times when innovations are widespread. Hence it is better for him to worry about his clothing and food, where does his income come from and where he spends it. Indeed we are afraid that by examining and discussing the conflicts between the companions his heart will lean towards innovation and he will play in the hand of Satan, and those that Allah ﷻ ordered him to love, seek forgiveness for and follow, he will start speaking ill of them, reviling and hating them, and walk upon a destructive path. The person who praises some of the companions and criticizes and degrades some, he is afflicted with a Fitnah (trial, turmoil) as love and seeking forgiveness for all companions is obligatory." (*Ash-Sharee'ah*: 5/2485, 2491)

There is no need to comment on this speech of Imam Abu Bakr Al-Aajurri; without any doubt the result of researching and repeating the conflicts between the companions is what he pointed to, and many scholars of this community have continuously warned against it.

IMAM AHMAD IBN HANBAL

You have seen earlier the statements of Imam Ahlus Sunnah, Imam Ahmad about those who revile the companions as a result of their conflicts and those who express hatred and rancour against them; now read his statements about those who discuss and repeat the conflicts between the companions.

Verily, Imam Ahmad ibn Ja'far ibn Ya'qub Abul 'Abbas Al-Istakhri in his creed of Ahlus Sunnah which he quoted from Imam Ahmad ibn Hanbal, wrote that the Imam said regarding the companions:

> Mention the qualities of all the companions of the Messenger of Allah ﷺ and abstain from mentioning their errors and the differences that occurred between them. Whoever insults one of the companions of the Messenger of Allah ﷺ or degrades him or reviles him or presents his defects and blames him, he is an innovator, a Rafidi, a filthy opponent, and no obligatory or voluntary action will be accepted from him. Contrary to this, loving them (the companions) is Sunnah and supplicating for them is an act of proximity (to Allah) and taking them as models is a Wasilah (intermediary) and following their footsteps is nobility... It is not permissible for anyone to mention any of their weaknesses or to degrade any of them with a defect or blame. Whoever does such, the ruler should reprimand and punish him and he should not forgive him, rather he should punish him and repentance should be sought from him. If he repents then it is accepted from him and if he perseveres, he is punished again, and he should remain in jail until he dies or repents from it. (*Tabaqat Al-Hanabilah* of Ibn Abi Ya'la: 1/30)

Likewise another student of Imam Ahmad, Imam Muhammad ibn Habeeb Al-Andarani quoted from him when mentioning the creed of Ahlus Sunnah wal Jama'ah: "Forgiveness is sought for all the companions of Muhammad ﷺ, their youngest and eldest, and mention their virtues and refrain from mentioning the conflicts between them." (*Tabaqat Al-Hanabilah:* 1/294)

Also when Imam Musaddad ibn Musarhad Al-Basri asked Imam Ahmad about the Fitnah (trial, turmoil) of I'tizal, Irja, Qadar and Rafd and the creed of Ahlus Sunnah, then in his detailed response, he wrote: "Refrain from mentioning the errors of the companions of the Messenger of Allah ﷺ, narrate their virtues and abstain from mentioning their conflicts." (*Tabaqat Al-Hanabilah:* 1/344)

Moreover, when Imam Abu Muhammad Rizqullah AbdulWahab At-Tamimi mentioned the creed of Imam Ahmad ibn Hanbal, he mentioned in it:

> He would forbid scrutinizing the conflicts between them and would say that one should not say except good and excellent praises about them... and he should abstain from scrutinizing the events that occurred at Siffin, Al-Jamal and say: "This is the blood that Allah protected my hands from touching, so I will protect my tongue from dwelling on it." (*Tabaqat Al-Hanabilah:* 2/272-273)

Imam Abdus ibn Malik Abu Muhammad Al-'Attar is among the students of Imam Ahmad. When he mentioned the creed of Ahlus Sunnah, he quoted Imam Ahmad saying about the companions that the best is Abu Bakr, then 'Umar and then Uthman ﷺ, and then the five members of the Shurah, then the people of Badr according to their precedence in Hijrah, and then the companions who were in his time and accompanied him for a year, a month, a day or an hour, those who had the honour to visit him. And those who spend the shortest of time among those who had the honour to visit him, they will be superior to those who were deprived of visiting him even if they were to meet Allah after spending their entire lives in doing good actions. Indeed those who spend an hour with him are better than all the Tabi'un (summarised from *Tabaqat Al-Hanabilah*: 1/243). This statement of Imam Ahmad clarifies the creed of Ahlus Sunnah on the great status of the companions and their conflicts.

Imam Ahmad was further asked about the dispute between Ali and Mu'awiyah ﷺ, and he turned away from it and quoted (the verse):

$$\text{تِلْكَ أُمَّةٌ قَدْ خَلَتْ لَهَا مَا كَسَبَتْ وَلَكُم مَّا كَسَبْتُمْ وَلَا تُسْأَلُونَ عَمَّا كَانُواْ يَعْمَلُونَ}$$

That is a nation which has passed on. It will have [the consequence of] what it earned, and you will have what you have earned. And you will not be asked about what they used to do. (Al-Baqarah: 141) (*Tabaqat Al-Hanabilah*: 1/97; *Sharh Fiqh Al-Akbar*, p71)

Imam Muhammad ibn Ahmad Abu 'Ali Al-Hashimi Al-Qadhi is counted among the senior students of Imam Ahmad. He mentioned the creed of Ahlus Sunnah saying:

> We do not research about their matters concerning their differences and we refrain from scrutinizing such reports and do not mention them except in the best of manners... we do not enter in their conflicts" (*Tabaqat Al-Hanabilah*: 2/185; *Al-Manhaj Al-Ahmad*: 2/117)

The statement of this foremost student of Imam Ahmad reflects and represents the view of Imam Ahmad as we have shown from previous quotes.

THE POSITION OF IMAM ABU HANIFAH

The book *Fiqh Al-Akbar* is counted among the books of Imam Abu Hanifah, though there is a difference among the people of knowledge regarding its attribution to him, many scholars declared it to be a writing of Imam Abu Hanifah. He said in this book: "We love them all and we do not mention the companions".

Allamah Ali Qari explained this sentence saying that one of the manuscripts contains such words at the end: "and we do not mention any of the companions of the Messenger of Allah ﷺ except with good". He further explained this quote:

> Meaning: that if something occurred from some of them which in its essence was evil, it was due to Ijtihad and was not corruption from the aspect of persisting or stubbornness, rather their ending was to return from it towards good based on good opinion about them. (*Sharh Fiqh Al-Akbar*, p71).

He wrote regarding the battle of Jamal: "The decision of Talhah and Zubayr ؤ was a mistake except that they did such based on Ijtihad" (*Sharh Fiqh Al-Akbar*, p67). Likewise he wrote about Mu'awiyah ؤ: "Then Mu'awiyah was mistaken except that he did such based on extrapolation (Ta'weel)."

Another scholar who explained *Al-Fiqh Al-Akbar*, Allamah Abul Muntaha Ahmad ibn Muhammad Al-Maghnisawi wrote:

> The creed of Ahlus Sunnah wal Jama'ah is to purify all the companions and praise them as Allah ﷻ and His Messenger ﷺ praised them, and what occurred between 'Ali and Mu'awiyah ؤ was based on Ijtihad." (*Sharh Al-Fiqh Al-Akbar*, published by Majmu'ah Rasail As-Sab'ah Hyderabad Deccan, 1948)

THE CLARIFICATION OF IMAM TAHAWI

Imam Abu Ja'far Muhammad ibn Muhammad Tahawi is the symbol of the creed of Imam Abu Hanifah; he wrote in his famous book *Al-Aqidah At-Tahawiyah*:

> We love the companions of the Messenger of Allah ﷺ, and we do not exaggerate in the love of any of them nor we disown any of them, and we hate those who hate them and speak ill of them, and we do not mention them except with good, and loving them is part of religion, part of faith

and part of perfection (Ihsan), and hating them is disbelief, hypocrisy and transgression" (*Sharh Al-Aqidah At-Tahawiyah*, p467)

We learn from this speech of Imam Tahawi that there should be no excess regarding the companions and neither should one disown them while the Rafidah exaggerate in their love of 'Ali ﷺ and free themselves from the other companions. We should love the companions but not disown any of them, and blaming and reviling any of them or launching a campaign of vilification against any of them is absolutely not the position of Ahlus Sunnah, rather with their love of them, they do not disown any of them.

The commentator of the creed of Tahawiyah explained the creed of the Salaf with the following words:

> Testifying is an innovation and disowning (Bara'ah) is an innovation. This has been narrated by a group among the Salaf from the companions and Tabi'un, and we count among them Abu Sa'eed Al-Khudri, Al-Hasan Al-Basri, Ibrahim An-Nakh'i, Ad-Dahak and others. The meaning of testifying is to testify that a particular person among the Muslims will go to hell or he is a disbeliever. (*Sharh Aqidah Tahawiyah*, pp470-471)

Rather Imam Ahmad ibn Hanbal would say:

> Disowning (Bara'ah) is an innovation, friendship (Wilayah) is an innovation and testifying (Shahadah) is an innovation. Disowning is to free from any of the companions of the Messenger of Allah ﷺ, Wilayah is to love some and abandon others, Shahadah is to testify for anyone that he will be in hell. (*As-Sunnah* of Al-Khallal, p479).

This saying makes it clear like daylight that the position of the Salaf is to love all the companions, and one should not disown any of them and no Muslim should be testified with going to hell. Disowning a companion, having animosity and rancour towards him, and reviling any of the companions are not from the signs of the Salaf but rather from the signs of the people of innovation. Imam Tahawi further writes:

> Whoever has a good speech regarding the companions of the Messenger of Allah ﷺ, regarding his wives, purified from any defect, and his saintly progeny, purified from any impurity, he has freed himself from hypocrisy." (*Sharh Al-Aqidah At-Tahawiyah*, p490)

This means that Ahlus Sunnah, avoid the excesses of the Rafidis and Nasibis, love all of the companions and always mention them with good. They are not likethe Nasibis who hold animosity and hatred towards 'Ali ﷺ and his family, which in reality is the family and progeny of the Prophet ﷺ. And they are not like Rafidis who disown all the companions except Ali ﷺ and revile and degrade them.

THE CLARIFICATION OF IMAM ABU ZUR'AH RAZI AND IMAM ABU HATIM RAZI

Imam Abu Muhammad AbdurRahman ibn Abi Hatim, the author of *Al-Jarh wa Ta'deel*, said in his book *Kitab Usul As-Sunnah wa Usul Ad-Din*:

> I asked my father (Abu Hatim Razi) and Abu Zur'ah about the school of though of Ahlus Sunnah regarding the fundamentals of the religion and the scholars of all cities whom they reached and their beliefs.

In their reply about the creed of Ahlus Sunnah, they mentioned the following words regarding the companions:

> And the ten which have been named by the Messenger of Allah ﷺ, and he testified paradise for them, they are according to his testimony, and his speech is truth. We should seek forgiveness for all the companions of Muhammad ﷺ and refrain from mentioning the conflicts between them. (*Usul As-Sunnah*, p20; *Sharh Usul I'tiqad* of Imam Al-Lalika'i: 1/177)

This epistle of Imam Ibn Abi Hatim has been published with the verification of Shaykh Muhammad Ozair Shams with other epistles by Ad-Daar As-Salafiyah Hind under the title *Rawa'id At-Turath*. Imam Al-Lalika'i, after few pages, quotes further from them:

> We seek forgiveness for all the companions of the Prophet ﷺ and who do not insult any of them due to His saying:

> رَبَّنَا ٱغْفِرْ لَنَا وَلِإِخْوَٰنِنَا ٱلَّذِينَ سَبَقُونَا بِٱلْإِيمَٰنِ وَلَا تَجْعَلْ فِى قُلُوبِنَا غِلًّا لِّلَّذِينَ ءَامَنُوا۟ رَبَّنَآ إِنَّكَ رَءُوفٌ رَّحِيمٌ

> **"Our Lord, forgive us and our brothers who preceded us in faith and put not in our hearts [any] resentment toward those who have believed. Our Lord, indeed You are Kind and Merciful."** (Al-Hashr: 10) (*Sharh Usul I'tiqad*: 1/181)

The creed of the Salaf mentioned by Imam Abu Zur'ah and Imam Abu Hatim Razi regarding the Sahabah and what Imam Lalika'i quoted from them regarding the fundamentals of Ahlus Sunnah, its first part has also been mentioned by Imam Abul 'Ala Al-Husayn ibn Ahmad Al-'Attar Al-Hamadani (d. 569 AH) in his epistle *Futya wa Jawabuha fi Zikr Al-I'tiqad wa Zam Al-Ikhtilaf* (pp90-94) and he called this part: "Fi Zikr Al-Itiqad lazi Ajma'a aleyhi Ullama Al-Bilad" (In the mention of the creed upon whoch the scholars of countries agreed upon). Shaykh Abdullah ibn Yusuf who verified this epistle mentioned that this creed of Imam Abu Zur'ah and Imam Abu Hatim has also been mentioned by Ibn At-Tabari in *As-Sunnah* (no. 321). This proves that the clarification of the creed of the Salaf regarding the companions written by these two scholars of Hadith has been relied upon by many Imams after them.

THE CREED OF IMAM BUKHARI AND HIS 1,080 TEACHERS

The leader of the jurist and scholars of Hadith Imam Muhammad ibn Isma'eel Bukhari (d 256H) before mentioning his creed said that he met more than more than a thousand teachers, and he did not meet them once but many times in different Islamic areas such as Hijaz, Makkah, Madeenah, Kufah, Basrah, Wasit, Baghdad, Shaam, Misr, and the Jazeerah and he met them one after the other for more than 46 years, and they all agreed that the religion is speech and action, the Quran is the speech of Allah and is not created, and other topics of creed. Among these matters of creed he wrote:

> And I have not seen any of them (my teachers) speaking ill of the companions of Muhammad ﷺ; A'ishah said: "They were ordered to seek forgiveness for them". (*Sharh Usul I'tiqad*: 1/175)

When Imam Bukhari mentioned his creed and different Muslim lands he visited, he also mentioned the names of some of his teachers. Hafiz ibn Hajar mentioned in *Hadi As-Sari* (p479) that the number of Imam Bukhari's teachers is 1,080. Mentioning the names of all of his teachers here will be too long, hence we will not go into details; our aim is to show that all these noble teachers agreed on the fact that one should always seek forgiveness for the noble companions and should not dare to tarnish their honour and nobility, but it is very unfortunate that some people in opposition to the Imams of the religion level blame and objections on the noble companions, rather they have the habit after mentioning the name of some of the companions to attribute defects to them and despite this they consider themselves as the symbols of Ahlus Sunnah wal Jama'ah wa Ahlul Hadith. Inna Lillahi wa Inna Ilayhi Rajiun!

THE CREED OF IMAM 'ALI IBN MADINI

The famous teacher of Imam Bukhari, the Muhadith and critic Imam Ali ibn Madini mentioned the creed of Ahlus Sunnah and said regarding the noble companions that the companion is the one who accompanied the Prophet ﷺ for one year, or one month, or one small period of time, and he had the honour to visit him, that the lowest among the companions is better than the best of the Tabi'un even if the Tabi'un did all actions of piety, and that Abu Bakr is the best among the companions, then Umar then Uthman ﷺ, after them the people of the Shura. After a few sentences, he said:

> Whoever reviles any of the companions of the Messenger of Allah ﷺ or hates any of them due to one of his action, or mentions his defects, he is an innovator until he seeks forgiveness for all of them so his heart will be sound towards all of them. (*Sharh Usul I'tiqad*: 1/169)

THE ADVICE OF IMAM GHAZALI

Imam Abu Hamid Muhammad ibn Muhammad Al-Ghazali (d. 505 AH) said in his famous book *Ihya Ulum*:

> The creed of Ahlus Sunnah is to purify all the companions (from defects) and praise them as Allah (ﷻ) and His Messenger ﷺ praised them, and what occurred between Mu'awiyah and 'Ali ﷺ was based on Ijtihad. (*Ihya Al-Ulum*: 1/120)

He mentioned after the type of Ijtihad of these two companions, that 'Ali ﷺ thought that taking the killers of 'Uthman ﷺ to account at the beginning of the establishment of his caliphate could weaken his caliphate as most of the killers were part of the Islamic army, hence he though that delaying this matter was appropriate, while Mu'awiyah ﷺ thought if the matter of the killers of 'Uthman ﷺ was delayed it would bring more bloodshed and the actions of those transgressing against the caliph will find sympathy, and hence he did not appreciate the delay in taking the killers of 'Uthman to account. This difference in Ijtihad resulted in the battle of Siffin, the position of 'Ali was without any doubt closer to the truth but we should not blame or revile Mu'awiyah ﷺ for his error in Ijtihad. This is what he explained in his book *Al-Iqtisad fil I'tiqad*. Allamah ibn Hajar Haytami Al-Makki quoted from Imam Ghazali that he said:

> It is forbidden for the orator or others to narrate the killing of Al-Husayn ﷺ and the conflicts and disputes that occurred between the companions

as it excites against some of the companions and may encourage one to revile them while they are illustrious personalities of the religion; the Imams of the religion took the religion from them through narrations, and we took it from the Imams of the religion in explanation. Hence the one blaming them has blamed his very essence and religion. (*As-Sawa'iq Al-Muharraqah*, p223)

The dangerous consequence of narrating the conflicts between the companions and making it a topic of discussion pointed to by Imam Ghazali is shown by the fruits and labours of those who write books claiming to verify and resolve (Tahqiq), but the details of such books are not our topic.

THE CREED OF IMAM IBN DAQEEQ AL-'EED

Allamah Ali Qari wrote about Imam Taqiudin Abul Fath Muhammad ibn Ali ibn Wahb ibn Daqeeq Al-'Eed (d. 702 AH):

Ibn Daqeeq Al-'Eed said in his creed: "The narrations about their conflicts and differences: some of them are falsehood and lies so one should not look at them, and some are authentic so we should interpret them in a good manner as the praise from Allah about them has preceded, so the speech narrated after is capable of being interpreted, and what is ambiguous and doubtful does not cancel what is verified and certain." (*Sharh Fiqh Al-Akbar*, p. 71)

THE CLARIFICATION OF QADHI 'IYADH

Qadhi 'Iyadh ibn Musa (d. 544 AH) wrote in his famous book *Ash-Shifa* about the companions, their virtues and the conflicts that occurred between them:

Part of respecting and obeying the Prophet ﷺ consists of respecting his companions, obeying them, recognising what is due to them, following them, praising them, asking forgiveness for them, refraining from discussing their differences, showing enmity to those who are hostile towards them and shunning the misguidance of the Shi'a and the innovators and the reports of any historians or ignorant transmitters who detract from any of them. If there is something equivocal which is reported about them regarding the turmoils that took place between them, then adopt the best interpretation and look for the most correct way out of it since that is what they deserve. None of them should be mentioned in a bad manner nor are they to be rebuked for anything. Rather, we mention their good deeds, their virtues and their praiseworthy lives and are silent about anything else. (*Ash-Shifa*: 2/41)[7]

After quoting few Ahadith, Qadhi 'Iyadh mentioned the statement of the famous Tabi'i Imam Ayub As-Sakhtiyani:

Whoever praises in an excellent manner the companions of Muhammad ﷺ, he has freed himself from hypocrisy, and whoever disparages any of them is an innovator opposing the Sunnah and the pious predecessors, and I fear that none of his good action will rise to the sky until he loves all of them and his heart is sound (towards them). (*Ash-Shifa*)

Also he quoted the statement of Sahl ibn Abdillah Tustari saying: "The one who doesn't respect the companions has not believed in the Messenger ﷺ." (*Ash-Shifa*) He also praised Mu'awiyah ؓ and Allamah Al-Khafaji wrote in explanation of it: "Whoever reviles Mu'awiyah ؓ, he is a dog among the dogs of hell" (*Nasim Ar-Riyadh*: 30/430) The Mujaddid (reviver) of the Brelwi school of thought Ahmad Raza Khan Brelwi in *Ahkam Ash-Shari'at* (p123) also quoted this statement of Allamah Khafaji.

THE STATEMENT OF SHAYKH ABDULQADIR JILANI

Shaykh AbdulQadir Jilani (d. 561 AH) said in his famous book *Ghuniyah At-Talibin* after mentioning the rightly guided caliphs:

As for his battle with Talhah, Az-Zubayr, 'A'ishah and Mu'awiyah ؓ, Imam Ahmad gave an unequivocal statement about refraining from speaking about them and from whatever differences, disputes and discontentment occurred between them as Allah (ﷻ) will remove such between them on the Day of Resurrection. (1/77)

Afterwards he wrote that that the reason behind the fight between them was also because those fighting Ali ؓ were asking for retaliation for the blood of 'Uthman ؓ and his killers were in the army of 'Ali: "All of them followed a

---

[7] Tr: This quote is taken from the English translation of *Shifa* by Aisha Bewley.

correct extrapolation (Ta'weel) and the best thing for us is to refrain from this and to leave such matters to Allah ﷻ and He is the best of judges." (*Ghuniyah At-Talibin*)

After mentioning the rule of Mu'awiyah ؓ, he said that following the death of 'Ali and the establishment of peace by Hasan ؓ, the rule of Mu'awiyah is established authentically and none can differ about it. After these statements clarifying the creed of Ahlus Sunnah regarding the noble companions, he said:

> Ahlus Sunnah are in agreement on the obligation to refrain from mentioning the conflicts between the companions and abstaining from mentioning their mistakes; rather one should present their virtues and noble qualities, and leave the differences that occurred between Ali, Talha, Az-Zubayr, 'A'ishah and Mu'awiya ؓ to Allah (ﷻ) as we mentioned before.

These statements of Shaykh AbdulQadir Jilani clarify the position of Ahlus Sunnah, and it is clear that those who have a contrary view to this and repeat these events and make them a topic of discussion, their way is not the way of Ahlus Sunnah, rather it is the way of the people of innovation. O Allah make us see the truth as truth and give us the favour to follow it and show us falsehood as false and give us the favour to avoid it!

THE STATEMENT OF IMAM AL-HARAMAYN

Imam Al-Haramayn AbdulMalik Al-Juwayni (d. 478 AH) said:
> Rather the truth is one as indeed Ali (may Allah illuminate his face) fought Mu'awiyah regarding the Imamah (leadership) and 'Ali was right and Mu'awiyah was mistaken ؓ and he was excused in his mistake due to the Prophet's ﷺ saying: "Whoever performs Ijtihad and is right will have two rewards and the one who performs Ijtihad and is mistaken, he will have a single reward." (*Mughith Al-Khalq*, p9)

This is indeed the creed of Ahlus Sunnah and those who do not consider Mu'awiyah ؓ to be excused but rather declare him to be a criminal, verily they themselves are criminals and oppose Ahlus Sunnah.

THE STATEMENT OF IMAM NAWAWI

Imam Muhiyudin Abu Zakariya Yahya ibn Sharf An-Nawawi (d. 676 AH) said in his *Sharh Sahih Muslim*:

> The school of thought of Ahlus Sunnah and people of truth is having a good opinion about [the companions] and refraining from mentioning the quarrels that occurred between them and to extrapolate from their fighting, that they are only Mujtahid scholars extrapolating and they did not desire sin in this worldly life; rather both sides believed they were upon the truth and the other side was transgressing so it was necessary to fight to make the latter return to the command of Allah, and some were correct in Ijtihad and some were mistaken and excused in their mistake as it was based on Ijtihad; there is no sin upon the Mujtahid when he errs, and 'Ali ﷺ was the one upon the truth in these fights. This is the school of thought of Ahlus Sunnah. The matters were confusing to the point that a group among the companions were puzzled about these and isolated from both sides and did not take part in these battles, and had they been certain of the truth, they would not stay away from helping 'Ali. (*Sharh Sahih Muslim*: 2/390, Kitab Al-Fitan, "Bab iza Iltaqa Al-Muslimani Bi Sayfihima")

What Allamah Nawawi mentioned here, he mentioned again in more detail the same position of Ahlus Sunnah at the beginning of "Kitab Fazail As-Sahabah" and the conclusion of which is:

> The caliphate of 'Ali ﷺ is authentic by consensus, he was the caliph of his time and there was no other caliphate. Mu'awiyah ﷺ was among the trustworthy, noble and virtuous companions, and the fight that occurred between them was based on a doubt and both believed that they were upon the truth and were upright, and were extrapolating over the battles and other similar matters, and none of these matters expel them from their integrity as they were all Mujtahid. They differed in these topics that were issues of Ijtihad in the same manner as other Mujtahids differ after them on topics such as Qisas (retaliation in kind) and others. These matters do not impute any defect to any of them. The reason behind their fights was that they were entangled in some matters which caused a difference in Ijtihad and resulted in the creation of three groups: One group believed that they were upon the truth and the other group was transgressing and it is necessary to fight the transgressing group. The second group contrary to them claimed that they were upon the truth and their opposing group was transgressing. The third group considered

this issue as difficult and did not give preponderance to any view so they isolated themselves, and if it had become apparent that one of the groups was upon the truth, they would not have remained behind from supporting it. So all these groups are excused and the people of truth agree on the fact that they are all upright and their narrations and testimonies are accepted. (*Sharh Muslim*: 2/272)

WHY MOST OF THE COMPANIONS REMAINED SEPARATE (FROM THE FIGHTS)?

Though Imam Nawawi declared that the reason for the third group for not participating in the fights was because the truth was not clear for them, another view which is closer to the truth is that they did not take part in the battles to avoid the Fitnah (trial, turmoil) as many texts interpreted internal fights as Fitnah. Hence most of the companions did not involve their hands in it. Indeed it is narrated with an authentic chain of narration from Imam Muhammad ibn Sirin that he said: "When the Fitnah occurred, the number of companions was 10,000, and 100, or rather approximately 30 among them participated in it" (*As-Sunnah* of Al-Khallal, p466).[8]

This statement of Imam Ibn Sirin has also been mentioned by Shaykh Al-Islam Ibn Taymiyah and he said about its chain of narration: "This chain of narration is from the most authentic chains on the surface of the earth" (*Minhaj*: 3/186). Likewise he said in another place:

> Most of the companions did not agree with the view of Ali ﷺ and many of them did not take a part in the battle, neither with him nor against him. Among the first forerunners Sa'd ibn Abi Waqqas, Abdullah ibn 'Umar, Usamah ibn Zayd, Muhammad ibn Maslamah and others ﷺ,

---

[8] Contrary to this, it is mentioned in *Tarikh Khaleefah ibn Khayat* (p194) and from it the words of Hafiz Dhahabi in *Tarikh Al-Islam* (1/445), that AbdurRahman ibn Abzi said that with Abdullah there were in Sifin 800 companions who had given the pledge of allegiance of Ridwan and 63 among them were martyred and Ammar ibn Yasir was among those martyred, but this saying is not authentic from the perspective of its chain of narration as Hafiz ibn Hajar said regarding its narrator Yazeed ibn AbdirRahman Abu Khalid Ad-Dalani: "Saduq, makes lots of mistakes and used to do Tadlees" (*Taqrib*, p584) and he reported this narration with the mode "'An" (from), hence this statement opposes the statement of Imam ibn Sirin and is not authentic.

though they loved 'Ali and considered him above others and considered him to be the most deserving of caliphate at this time, they did not agree with Ali on the issue of fighting. They had some religious texts that they heard from the Messenger of Allah ﷺ which indicated that avoiding taking part in the battle and fighting was better than participating in it and some of these religious texts clearly prohibit joining such battles. Such narrations and Athaar are famous. (*Minhaj*: 3/221)

Shaykh Al-Islam spoke about these issues in many places in *Minhaj As-Sunnah*, for those who desire to read them, see 4/180-181, 2/243, 205, 219, 220, 241 and 246. Among the companions who did not participate in these battles, we count Muhammad ibn Maslamah ﷺ, about whom the Prophet ﷺ said: "The Fitnah will not harm him". Shaykh Al-Islam ibn Taymiyah wrote:

> And this is from what was taken as evidence to say that this fighting was a fighting of Fitnah due to extrapolation, and it was neither a compulsory Jihad nor a recommended. (*Minhaj*: 4/17)

Ali ﷺ had asked Hakam ibn Amr Ghifari ﷺ to help him and he excused himself saying: "I heard my close friend (the Prophet) ﷺ saying that when the matter is as such, take a wooden sword" (*Hakim*: 3/442; *As-Siyar*: 2/475). Imran ibn Husayn ﷺ, who did not take part in these battles, said that it is forbidden to sell weapons during the days of Fitnah (*Bukhari* with *Fath*: 4/322, 323).

> The commentator on *Tahawiyah* said:
>
> When the major companions heard the religious texts commanding to sit and isolate during turmoils, they chose to stay away from these battles. They also considered that there would be little benefit by participating in them and more harms. We should remember all of them with good words. (*Sharh Aqidah At-Tahawiyah*, p484)

Shah Waliyullah Muhadith Dehlwi said:

> And there remains a very subtle point and the feet of many trip on this issue, and it is: Were the companions who stayed away from helping Murtadha (i.e. Ali ﷺ) Mujtahid who were correct or Mujtahid who were mistaken and excused? According to me the verified position is that those who chose to stay away chose the highest position and they took evidences from clear Ahadith which are authentic and Mutawatir in meaning. (*Izalah Al-Khafa*, translated edition, 4/526)

After this Shah Waliyullah Dehlwi mentioned the Ahadith he aluded to, and according to his particular style he replied to objections on such a view. We cannot here mention the detail of such, the aim was to show that that those who preferred to remain silent in these battles were great in number and their view was based on Prophetic Ahadith and it was correct. There was no issue that the truth was not clear to them as it was understood by Allamah Nawawi and others.

Hafiz Dhahabi mentioned regarding this a strange dream of Husayn ibn Kharijah Ashja'i. Ashja'i said:

> After the martyrdom of Uthman ﷠, I invoked Allah ﷻ to show me the path of truth; thus one day I saw in a dream the scenes of this world and the hereafter while I was on a wall and I met angels. I asked them: "Where are the martyrs?" and they said to me: "Go upstairs" so I went upstairs and met the Prophet ﷺ and Ibrahim ﵟ. The Prophet ﷺ asked Ibrahim ﵟ to invoke for forgiveness for his community, but he (Ibrahim ﵟ) said: "You don't know what they did after you, they spread bloodshed and martyred their Imam, why didn't they do like my close friend Sa'd ibn Abi Waqqas did?" Ashja'i said that he went to meet Sa'd ibn Abi Waqqas after and he expressed happiness after hearing this event and said: "The one whose close friend is not Ibrahim, this person is in loss". Ashja'i asked him: "Which of the two groups did you support?" and he replied: "I was not supporting any of them". I asked him "What do you command me to do?", and he replied: "Do you have sheep?" And I said: "No", and he said: "Buy some sheep and live with them until your end nears." (*As-Siyar*: 1/120)

This pious dream also supports those who chose to remain isolated from wars that their view was correct, preponderant and according to religious texts, as was expressed by Shaykh Al-Islam Ibn Taymiyah and Shah Waliyullah Muhadith Dehlwi.

THE CLARIFICATION OF SHAYKH AL-ISLAM IBN TAYMIYAH

Shaykh Al-Islam Imam Taqiyudin Abul 'Abbas Ahmad ibn AbdilHaleem (d. 728 AH) said in *Aqidah Al-Wasitiyah* in explaining the creed and principles of Ahlus Sunnah:

From the fundamentals of Ahlus Sunnah wal Jama'ah is to keep their hearts and tongues safe towards the companions of the Messenger ﷺ as Allah (ﷻ) described them in His speech:

رَبَّنَا ٱغْفِرْ لَنَا وَلِإِخْوَٰنِنَا ٱلَّذِينَ سَبَقُونَا بِٱلْإِيمَٰنِ وَلَا تَجْعَلْ فِى قُلُوبِنَا غِلًّا لِّلَّذِينَ ءَامَنُواْ رَبَّنَآ إِنَّكَ رَءُوفٌ رَّحِيمٌ

"Our Lord, forgive us and our brothers who preceded us in faith and put not in our hearts [any] resentment toward those who have believed. Our Lord, indeed You are Kind and Merciful." (Al-Hashr: 10) (*Al-Aqidah Al-Wasitiyah*, p111)

After mentioning this principle of Ahlus Sunnah, he mentioned the virtues of the rightly guided caliphs, the first forerunners, the household and wives of the Prophet ﷺ, and said:

And they disassociate themselves from the path of the Rawafid, those who hate the Companions and abuse them, and the path of the Nawasib, those who harm the members of the Household, either by their statements or by their actions. And they refrain from whatever disputes transpired among the Companions. And they say: These reports that are narrated regarding their shortcomings, among them are lies, and among them is that which contains additions, deletions, and alterations from their true state. And what is authentic from that, they are excused, either they made Ijtihad and were correct, or they made Ijtihad and were mistaken. They, with that, do not believe that each one of the Companions was protected from the major sins and the minor, rather, it is possible that they had sinned in general. And they possessed precedence and virtues warranting pardon for whatever occurred from them- if it did, such that He pardons from their shortcomings that He would not pardon for those after them, because they have such Hasanat that supersede our shortcomings, such that are not possessed by those after them... (p116; *Majmu Fatawa*: 3/152-155)[9]

The creed of Ahlus Sunnah explained by Shaykh Al-Islam is the same as what the ancient noble Imams have said in different words, implying any word

---

[9] Tr: Taken from the English translation by Darussalam with slight modifications.

containing the slightest degradation is a sign of the people of innovation and remaining silent regarding their differences is the way of Ahlus Sunnah.

Shaykh Al-Islam ibn Taymiyah explained in detail in another of his famous books, *Minhaj As-Sunnah An-Nabawiyyah fi Naqdh Kalam Ash-Shi'ah wal Qadariyah*" the position of the Salaf regarding the wars between the companions:

> It is from the school of thought of Ahlus Sunnah to refrain from mentioning the conflicts between the companions as their virtues are proven and loving them and taking them as friends has been made compulsory, and what occurred from them, they have an excuse which is hidden to others for some of these matters and for some others the authors of some actions might have repented and for some of these matters, they might be forgiven; so scrutinizing the conflicts that occurred generates in the souls of many hatred and blame towards them, so the person will, by doing such, be in error, rather he will be a sinner who harms his self, and the one who joined him in scrutinizing such as most of the people who speak about it, they end up speaking with words which is not beloved by Allah and His Messenger ﷺ, such as blaming someone with something that does not deserve a blame or praising someone for something that does not deserve praise, hence refraining from speaking was the way of the best among Salaf. (*Minhaj As-Sunnah*: 2/219-220)

While clarifying the view of the Salaf regarding the conflicts between the companions, the dangers towards which he pointed to, every person of reason can see it with his eyes and hear it through his ears given to him by Allah:

إِنَّ فِي ذَٰلِكَ لَذِكْرَىٰ لِمَن كَانَ لَهُۥ قَلْبٌ أَوْ أَلْقَى ٱلسَّمْعَ وَهُوَ شَهِيدٌ

Indeed in that is a reminder for whoever has a heart or who listens while he is present [in mind]. (Qaf 50: 37)

The same view of the Salaf is present in many other places (of Shaykhul Islam's books) but our aim is not to encompass all these places, those who which to read more can see *Minhaj As-Sunnah*: 2/205, *Majmu' Al-Fatawa*: 3/406 and *As-Sarim Al-Maslul*.

THE STATEMENT OF IMAM SABUNI

Shaykh Al-Islam Imam Abu Uthman Isma'eel ibn AbdirRahman As-Sabuni (d. 449 AH) while mentioning the creed of Ahlus Sunnah wrote in his epistle: *'Aqidah As-Salaf wa Ashab Al-Hadith* which is also known as *Ar-Risalah fi I'tiqad Ahlus Sunnah wa Ashabul Hadith wal A'imah"*:

> They believe in refraining from mentioning the conflicts between the companions of the Messenger of Allah ﷺ, and purifying their tongues from mentioning what contains a defect or a shortcoming in them, and they believe in seeking mercy for all of them and loving all of them, and likewise they believe in respecting the status of the wives of the Prophet ﷺ, in invoking for them, knowing their virtues and accepting that they are "mothers of the believers." (*Aqidah As-Salaf*, p93)

This book of Imam Sabuni is also published in *Rasail Majmu'ah Muniriyah* (1/129-130).

THE VIEW OF ALLAMAH IBN HAZM

Imam Abu Muhammad Ali ibn Hazm (d. 456 AH) said praising the companions and mentioning their high status:

> Paying respect to them and having esteem of them is obligatory upon us as well as to seek forgiveness for them and to love them. A single date donated by one of them is superior to the donation of one of us of what he possesses. The single sitting of one of them with the Prophet ﷺ is better than the worship of one of us during a whole lifetime, and this applies to all of them who were in his era whether they were young or adult. (*Al-Ahkam fi Usul Al-Ahkam*: 5/89)

The scholars of the community agree on the integrity of the noble companions and Allamah Ibn Hazm annihilated the foundations upon which the innovators base themselves on and spread their doubts and suspicions, by saying (in summary):

> Likewise those who fought Ali ﷺ on the Day of Siffin, they all had extrapolations. As for the people of Jamal, they did not intend to fight Ali and neither Ali had the intention to fight them, they only gathered to discuss about the killers of Uthman ﷺ and seeking the verdict of Allah (i.e. Qisas) for them; when the killers of Uthman ﷺ felt that the verdict of Allah would be applied on them, there were many thousands and they

stirred up the fight and when the battle started, each side was forced to defend itself, and this matter is clearly mentioned in historical narrations. It is extremely surprising that they declare the rulings based on Ijtihad of Imam Abu Hanifah, Imam Awza'i, Imam Layth, Imam Sufyan, Imam Ahmd and Imam Dawud correct on the issue of Qisas, Hudud and dealings, while if one Imam declares Qisas and Hadd legislated on an issue, another will deny it, one will declare some wealth as illicit and another will declare it licit, one will declare a person's blood licit and another will declare it illicit, one will declare an action to be obligatory and the other will declare its obligation removed, so there is a huge difference in their Ijtihad and we find room for it and consider them as excused. We believe that they are great Imams of the religion and we respect and honour them but we do not declare them with certainty to be from the people of paradise and with certainty that Allah is satisfied with them, though due to good opinion about them we hope such from Allah about them, so when our belief is such regarding the Imams of the religion, why is such not permissible for the companions?

And then shall we not allow such for Ali, the mother of the believer (Aishah), Talhah, Az-Zubayr, Ammar, Hisham ibn Hakeem, Mu'awiyah, Amr, An-Nu'man, Samurah, Abu Ghadiyah and others ﷺ, when they are the Imams of Islam in reality and their virtue is certain and for most of them paradise is certain? This opinion (of not allowing Ijtihad for Sahabah) cannot be thought of except by someone rejected. And all those we mentioned as correct and mistaken, they are rewarded for their Ijtihad, either with a double reward or a single reward, and none of this expels them from their integrity. (*Al-Ahkam*: 2/85-86)

While defending the noble companions from the verbal attacks of the innovators due to their internal fights, Allamah Ibn Hazm proved that such events do not affect their integrity, and moreover, he clarified the position of Ahlus Sunnah that one should overlook their disputes and have a clear love for them, and we should keep seeking forgiveness for them and always respect them and hold them in high esteem. Hafiz Ibn Hazm also discussed this topic in his book *Al-Fasl fil Milal wal Ahwa wa Nihal* (4/158,161) and those wishing to read it can refer to *Al-Fasl*.

THE ANALYSIS OF ALLAMAH IBN KHALDUN

The philosopher of Islamic history Allamah AbdurRahman ibn Muhammad ibn Khaldun gives his analysis regarding the dispute between Ali and Muawiyah ﷺ in his *Muqaddimah*:

> When the Fitnah occurred between Ali and Mu'awiyah ﷺ, and though it was the consequence of Al-'Asabiyah (partisanship), their decisions in it were based on truth and Ijtihad. Their fighting was not for material gains or preferring the spread of falsehood or based on a sense of jealousy and hatred as the delusional person might think in his delusions or the heretic might be inclined to. Their Ijtihad only differed in discerning the truth and both sides saw the other as discredited due to his Ijtihad in seeking the truth, hence they fought based on it. Though Ali ﷺ was correct in this, Mu'awiyah ﷺ did not intend to seek falsehood and he only intended to seek the truth and erred, and both of them were correct in their intentions. (*Muqadidmah ibn Khaldun*, p205, "Al-Fasl 28")

After reading extensively books of history and biographies, the analysis presented by Allamah Ibn Khaldun regarding the battles of the companions is what every Muslim should think and this is the position of the Salaf as you can read throughout this book.

THE STATEMENT OF ALLAMAH IBN KATHEER

The famous scholar of Tafsir, historian, Imam Abul Fida Imadudin Isma'eel ibn Katheer (d. 774 AH) wrote, when mentioning Mu'awiyah ﷺ:

> Then what happened between him and Ali ﷺ after the murder of Uthman ﷺ was based on Ijtihad and Rai (opinion such as analogical reasoning) and a great battle occurred between them as we have mentioned previously, and the truth and correct position was with Ali ﷺ and Mu'awiyah ﷺ was excused according to the majority of ancient and recent scholars. (*Al-Bidayah*: 8/126)

Imam Ibn Katheer explained this in another place as follows:

This Hadith[10] is among the proofs of Prophethood, and the events occurred as he ﷺ informed, and it contains the ruling of Islam on both sides: the people of Shaam and the people of Iraq, not as thought by the sects of the Rafidah and ignorant and transgressing people who excommunicate the people of Shaam. This Hadith also indicates that the side of Ali ؓ was the closest to the truth among the two groups, and this is the view of the school of thought of Ahlus Sunnah, that Ali ؓ was correct though Mu'awiyah ؓ was a Mujtahid and he will be rewarded insha Allah...

Likewise Hafiz Ibn Katheer said regarding the Hadith about the construction of Masjid Nabawwi which states about Ammar ؓ: "The transgressing group will kill you" that this Hadith is among the proofs of the Prophet's ﷺ veracity, as Ammar ؓ was killed by the people of Shaam and he was with Ali ؓ:

> Calling the companions of Mu'awiyah ؓ "transgressors (Bughat)" does not entail their excommunication as the ignorant people of the misguided sects from the Shi'ah and others try to claim, for even though there were transgressors in the matter, they were exerting Ijtihad in their engaging in the battle, and not every Mujtahid is correct, but rather the correct one receives two rewards and the mistaken one receives a single reward. (*Al-Bidayah*: 3/218)

Hafiz Ibn Katheer did not leave any ambiguity regarding the position of Ahlus Sunnah, Muawiyah ؓ was a "Baghi" (rebel), but not such as one who is perverted or corrupt, but rather as one who is rewarded by Allah, and at the end Hasan ؓ, by abandoning his caliphate and rule, established peace with Mu'awiyah ؓ and the Prophet ﷺ praised and approved this peace through prophecy. Indeed Abu Bakrah ؓ narrated that the Messenger of Allah ﷺ said about Hasan ؓ: "This son of mine is a leader, maybe Allah through him will establish peace between two factions of the Muslims" (*Bukhari*: 1/530 and others).

---

[10] Tr: The hadith in *Sahih Muslim* reads: "A dissenting faction will splinter at a time of disunity between the Muslims, and they will be fought by the more correct of the two parties". The party of Ali fought the Khawarij in the Battle of Nahrawan in the year 37 AH, hence the party closer to the truth is Ali's army.

And it occurred as such. Six months after the martyrdom in 41 AH, Mu'awiyah and Hasan ﷺ concluded a peace agreement and this year was called "The year of the group ('Aam Al-Jama'ah)" and this prophecy of the Prophet ﷺ came true. This makes it clear that the saying "Baghi" regarding the people of Shaam was a point of view related to an incident and was in the context of the opposition to Ali ﷺ, and it has no link to disbelief and Islam, and this reality has been expressed also by Ali ﷺ for he wrote to different cities saying:

> And it is apparent that our Lord is one and our call to Islam is one and we are not superior to them in faith in Allah and in attesting to the truth of His Messenger ﷺ and neither are they superior to us in this; our matter is one except what we differ in about the blood of Uthman ﷺ and we are free from it..." (*Nahj Al-Balaghah*: 3/114 and with it, *Ibn Abi Al-Hudayr*: 4/161)

Rather the view of Ali ﷺ regarding the Battles of the Camel and Siffin will be detailed ahead in this book. So in opposition to these realities, taking the word "Baghi" to mean disbelief from Islam or perversion of corruption is absolutely incorrect and a result of animosity towards the companions.

THE CLARIFICATION OF IMAM IBN ATHEER

Imam Majdudin Al-Mubarak ibn Muhammad ibn Atheer Al-Jawzi (d. 606 AH) said in the introduction of his famous book *Jami' Al-Usul*, while discussing different topics under the heading "Al-Far' Ath-Thalith fi Bayan Tabaqat Al-Majruhin" that the view of the Mu'tazilah, Qadariyah and other sects of innovators is that those who made moves against Ali ﷺ, such as Aishah, Talhah, Az-Zubayr, Mu'awiyah and others ﷺ are corrupt (Fasiq), and some of these sects even said the same about Ali and Uthman ﷺ! He wrote refuting these sects:

> All of this daring speech upon the Salaf is contrary to the Sunnah, as what occurred between them was based on Ijtihad, and every Mujtahid is correct (meaning he strives to arrive at a correct judgement) and the one who is correct is one and he is rewarded and the one who is mistaken is excused, his testimony is not rejected. (*Jami' Al-Usul*: 1/133)

What we derive from this is clear, declaring those who fought Ali ﷺ as corrupt is not the view of Ahlus Sunnah but rather the view of the innovators.

THE POSITION OF ALLAMAH IBN ABIL 'IZZ

The commentator of *Al-Aqidah At-Tahawiyah,* Allamah Sadrudin Muhammad ibn Ala Ad-Din Ali ibn Muhammad ibn Abil 'Izz Ad-Dimashqi (d. 792 AH) said under the mention of Ali ﷺ:

> We say good about all of them;
>
> رَبَّنَا ٱغْفِرْ لَنَا وَلِإِخْوَٰنِنَا ٱلَّذِينَ سَبَقُونَا بِٱلْإِيمَٰنِ وَلَا تَجْعَلْ فِى قُلُوبِنَا غِلًّا لِّلَّذِينَ ءَامَنُوا۟ رَبَّنَآ إِنَّكَ رَءُوفٌ رَّحِيمٌ
>
> **"Our Lord, forgive us and our brothers who preceded us in faith and put not in our hearts [any] resentment toward those who have believed. Our Lord, indeed You are Kind and Merciful." (Al-Hashr: 10)**
>
> The Turmoil that occurred at his time, Allah has protected our hands from it, so I ask Allah that He protects our tongues from it by His grace and mercy. (*Sharh Al-Aqidah,* p484)

THE STATEMENT OF HAFIZ DHAHABI

The historian of Islam Hafiz Abu Abdillah Muhammad ibn Ahmad ibn Uthman Dhahabi (d. 748 AH) wrote while explaining the methodology of Ahlus Sunnah:

> The people of the first generation after the event of Siffin were divided into different groups; Ahlus Sunnah - and they are the people of knowledge-, they love the companions and refrain from scrutinizing what occurred between the companions, such as Sa'd, ibn Umar, Muhammad ibn Maslamah and a group. (*Siyar A'lam An-Nubala*: 5/374)

Afterwards he mentioned the views of the Rafidis and Nasibis and it is not necessary to mention the details of their views here. Mu'awiyah ibn Hudayj differed with Ali ﷺ and would say unsuitable words about him so Hafiz Dhahabi said about this:

> There occurred between the two sides of Siffin something more than Sabb (reviling, abusing, insulting), indeed it led to the sword, and if something regarding this is authentic then our way is to refrain from speaking and seek forgiveness for the companions, and we do not love whatever conflicts occurred between them and we seek Allah's refuge from such, and we love the leader of the believers Ali ﷺ. (*As-Siyar*: 3/39)

Meaning: if one of the sides said something bad about the other side then it is a matter between them, and the matter between them went above words as it led to the sword, but we should remain silent absolutely and seek forgiveness for all of them.

THE CLARIFICATION OF ALLAMAH SUBKI

Allamah Tajudin AbdulWahab ibn Ali As-Subki (d. 771 AH), while discussing the integrity of the companions, mentioned the conflicts between the companions and the conclusion of his speech is:

> We relegate the matters between [the companions] to Allah ﷻ and we free ourselves in front of Him from those who revile and degrade them. Our belief is that the one who reviles them is misguided and in evident loss. Also our belief is that Uthman ؓ was a truthful Imam and he was martyred unjustly and Allah preserved all companions from participating in his assassination[11]. The one who killed him was an extremist devil and it is not proven that any of the companions expressed satisfaction at his murder; rather condemnation of it is established from them. Afterwards the issue of the Qisas (retaliation) of Uthman ؓ was an Ijtihadi matter,

---

[11] The words of Allamah Subki "Min Mubasharah Qatlihi" (from participating in his assassination) indicates that the noble companions did not participate by action in the assassination of Uthman ؓ, and this view is more closer to the truth compared to the view that there were no companions among those who took steps against Uthman ؓ. Indeed, some companions were influenced by the Fitnah of the followers of Abdullah ibn Saba and they participated in the movement of Abdullah ibn Saba against Uthman ؓ in the same manner as some sincere companions were affected by the poisonous campaign of the head of the hypocrites Abdullah ibn Ubay against Aishah ؓ. Among these companions we count AbdurRahman ibn Udays who participated in the oath of allegiance of Ridhwan about whom the Prophet ﷺ said: "None of the people who gave oath of allegiance under the tree will enter the fire". (*Sahih Muslim*; *As-Saheehah*: 2160). After this authentic statement of the Prophet ﷺ, our creed and faith is that he and other companions who took part in the Fitnah and Fasad (turmoil and tumult) against Uthman ؓ are certainly forgiven due to any causes that brings forgiveness, and they won't be taken to task by Allah. Ibn 'Udays was affected by this Fitnah but it is not established with any authentic chain of narration that he participated in the assassination of Uthman ؓ. Likewise what is narrated about 'Amr ibn Al-Hamq participating in the killing of Uthman is narrated by Al-Waqidi (*Tabaqat Ibn Sa'd*: 3/73) and Al-Waqidi is not relied upon by the scholars of Hadith.

Ali ⚔ believed that there was a benefit in delaying it and Aishah ⚔ believed that there is benefit in taking Qisas (retaliation) early, and both of them acted upon their Ijtihad and insha Allah both of them deserve reward.

After Uthman ⚔, the truthful Imam was Ali and Mu'awiyah and his companions were extrapolating, and there were some companions who isolated themselves from both sides as the matter was ambiguous for them thus they did not join any sides ⚔. All of them applied Ijtihad, all of them were upright, transmitters of the religion and upheld the religion. Verily the religion became preponderant through their swords and through their tongues Islam spread. If we were to recite the verses and read the Ahadith regarding their virtues, it would take us a long time, so such short words are such that if someone has a creed opposing it then he will be involved in misguidance and innovation. The religious person should put a knot on it and prevent his tongue from whatever occurred between the companions. This is the blood from which Allah preserved our hands so we should not let our tongues be sullied. (As quoted in *Tahrir Al-Usul ma'a Sharh Taqrir Al-Usul*: 2/260-261)

Allamah Subki indicated that this is the creed of Ahlus Sunnah regarding the companions, and this clarification has preceded from many noble Imams, but like Imam Nawawi, his statement that the third group isolated itself from these wars due to the matter being ambiguous is disputable, as this group was more numerous and their staying away from fighting was due to seeking safety from Fitnah (trial, turmoil) as we explained earlier, Allah knows best.

THE STATEMENT OF ALLAMAH AL-AAMIDI

Allamah Sayfudin Abul Hasan Ali ibn Abi Ali Muhammad Al-Aamidi (d. 631 AH) said in his book *Al-Ahkam fi Usul Al-Ahkam,* after discussing the topic of the integrity of the companions and mentioning in detail the views of the innovators:

Thus it is obligatory to consider the turmoil which occurred between them in the best light and if such occurred it only resulted from the Ijtihad of each side, that his belief was what was obligatory to follow and that it was better for the religion and more correct for the Muslims. (*Al-Ahkam*: 2/129-130)

Contrary to this, attacking the companions and holding them as guilty is not a service to the religion and nor is a good perspective of good for the Muslims found in it. Some people with their naivety and lack of knowledge publicise these events in a repetitive manner to the ears of Muslims and some claimants of knowledge and deep understanding mention these events with excitement and think that they are busy in a great service to Islam. Doing such is a terrible fraud:

$$ يُخَٰدِعُونَ ٱللَّهَ وَٱلَّذِينَ ءَامَنُواْ وَمَا يَخْدَعُونَ إِلَّآ أَنفُسَهُمْ وَمَا يَشْعُرُونَ $$

They [think to] deceive Allah and those who believe, but they deceive not except themselves and perceive [it] not. (Baqarah: 9)

THE STATEMENT OF HAFIZ IBN HAJAR

Hafiz Ad-Duniya Imam Abul Fadl Ahmad ibn Ali ibn Muhammad ibn Hajar Al-Asqalani (d. 852 AH) said in *Al-Isabah fi Tamyiz As-Sahabah*:

> Our opinion of the companions during these wars is that they were extrapolating in these issues, and the Mujtahid who errs will have a single reward and whereby this is proven for anyone among the people, the companions are more deserving of this. (*Al-Isabah*: 7/148)

Hence if a companion errs in his Ijtihad, he will deserve a single reward and he will not be accounted for it and the details of this have been mentioned previously in the speech of Hafiz Ibn Hazm. Hafiz Ibn Hajar wrote in another place:

> Ahlus Sunnah are in agreement on the obligation of forbidding the revilement of any of the companions due to what happened between them from these (wars) even if he knows who was right in them, as they did not fight these wars except by Ijtihad and Allah ﷻ has forgiven the mistaken one in his Ijtihad, rather it is established that he will have a single reward and the one who is correct will have two rewards. (*Fath Al-Bari:* 13/34)

Likewise he wrote in another place:

> And the majority of Ahlus Sunnah went to declare correct those who fought alongside Ali ؓ by following the verse
>
> $$ وَإِن طَآئِفَتَانِ مِنَ ٱلْمُؤْمِنِينَ ٱقْتَتَلُواْ $$
>
> **"If two factions among the believers should fight..."** (Al-Hujurat 49:9)

And it contains the order to fight the transgressing group (Al-Fiah Al-Baghiyah), and it is proven that those who fought against Ali ﷺ were transgressors (Bughat), and they, according to this declaration of correctness (in favour of the side of Ali ﷺ) are in agreement that none of those (who transgressed) should be blamed, rather it is said that they performed Ijtihad and erred... (*Fath Al-Bari:* 13/67)

Hafiz Ibn Hajar explained the school of thought of Ahlus Sunnah is that the position of Ali ﷺ was correct regarding the affairs between the companions, but this does not necessitate that the other companions should be blamed or reviled, rather they will be considered as rewarded due to being mistaken Mujtahidun and they will be excused.

THE STATEMENT OF HAFIZ SAKHAWI

Allamah Abu Abdillah ibn AbdirRahman As-Sakhawi (d. 902 AH), while discussing the integrity of the companions, wrote that Allamah Al-Maziri said in his *Sharh Al-Burhan* that when we say that all the companions are upright, it means those companions who had a long companionship and participated in Jihad with the Prophet ﷺ during difficult times and defended him, but no one except Allamah Al-Maziri said this. Allamah Al-'Ala'i said that this view is strange and if it was to be adopted then Waail ibn Hujr, Malik ibn Al-Huwairith, Uthman ibn Abil 'Aas and others ﷺ who came in a group to visit the Prophet ﷺ and remained with him for a little period of time before returning or those who reported only one or two narrations, their integrity would be dismissed. Commenting on this view, as-Sakhawi wrote:

> In conclusion, what Al-Maziri said is criticised, rather everything outside the first school of thought which encompasses all (companions in integrity) is falsehood and the first one is authentic, rather the correct view and the one which is taken into account, the majority of scholars are upon it as stated by Al-Aamidi, Ibn Al-Haajib and they intend the majority of the Salaf and those who came after them. And Al-Aamidi added that this is the chosen view, and Ibn AbdilBarr narrated in *Al-Isti'ab* a consensus of the people of truth among the Muslims, and they are the Ahlus Sunnah wal Jama'ah, on this matter (that the companions are all upright), whether they did not participate in the turmoil or participated, and in having a good opinion about them and considering what happened between them as based on Ijtihad. Indeed all these

matters are based on Ijtihad, and all Mujtahidun are correct or the correct Mujtahid is one and the mistaken is excused, even rewarded... (*Fath Al-Mughith*: 4/100)

Rather he said before this: "Rather abstaining from scrutinising such matters is what is incumbent". Likewise he said in the section of "Adaab Al-Muhadith" quoting from Khateeb Al-Baghdadi that we should avoid mentioning the internal conflicts between the companions. (*Fath Al-Mughith:* 3/269) Furthermore he said in another of his famous books, *I'lan bi Tawbikh man Zamma At-Tarikh* (p64): "We have received the command to abstain from what occurred between [the companions]".

THE STATEMENT OF ALLAMAH IBN AL-HUMMAM

Allamah Kamal Ad-Din Muhammad ibn AbdilWahid ibn Al-Humam (d. 861 AH) said in *Sharh Musamarah*:

> The creed of Ahlus Sunnah is to purify all the companions ؓ as an obligation due to Allah establishing it for all of them, and to refrain from reviling them, and to praise them as Allah ﷻ and His Messenger ﷺ praised them. And the battles that occurred between Mu'awiyah and Ali ؓ were based on Ijtihad and were not a dispute over leadership. (*Al-Musamarah bi Sharh Al-Musayrah*: 6/132; Deoband, p314)

ALLAMAH IBN AL-'ARABI'S VERDICT

Qadhi Abu Bakr Muhammad ibn Abdillah ibn Muhammad ibn Al-Arabi (d. 549 AH) said in *Ahkam Al-Quran,* while discussing the factors behind the battles between the companions, that these differences occurred due to Ijtihad:

> Each of the two sides were praising their companions and attesting paradise for them and mentioning their virtues, and if the matter was different from such, they would have disowned the other side. So the people were not fighting based on religion or transgression between them in creed, it was only due to differences in Ijtihad and this is the reason why all of them will be in paradise. (*Ahkam Al-Quran*: 2/224)

Likewise he wrote in his decisive book:

> Each one among them was a great Mujtahid and whatever they did was correct and they will be rewarded for it. This was the decision of Allah which occurred and Allah has already decided about it, so you have to reflect on these matters from the perspective of destiny. Have the same opinion about them as was chosen by Ibn Abbas and Ibn Umar, and do not become like those idiotic people who have let their tongues and pens free in discussions that have no benefit, and engaging in such things brings no benefit in this world or in the hereafter. Look at the greatest of Imams and jurists from different cities; have they paid attention to such fairy tales and idiotic matters? Rather they said that engaging in discussing such matters brings only partisanship of ignorance and support for falsehood. And aside from sectarianism, divergences and pursuit of desires, it does not bring any benefit. Whatever was to happen happened and whatever the historians had to say, they said it, so either remain silent or follow the people of knowledge and abandon the historians and writers, may Allah complete His mercy upon us and you. (The Urdu translation of *Al-Awasim min Al-Qawasim*, pp372-373)

Allamah Ibn Al-'Arabi, in his discussion in *Al-'Awasim*, clarified the points of view of Uthman, Aishah, Talhah, Zubayr and Mu'awiyah 🙵, and he replied to objections made against them. Within this discussion he also had some odd deductions but regarding the conflicts, his position is according to Ahlus Sunnah, as you have read in many statements of great Imams above: silence regarding their differences is the best of options. Mentioning these differences on pulpits is synonymous with bringing division within the community and spreading suspicion about the companions, may Allah 🕮 preserve us from such!

THE STATEMENT OF 'ALLAMAH IBN HAJAR HAYTAMI

'Allamah Ahmad ibn Muhammad ibn Ali ibn Hajar Al-Haytami Al-Makki (d. 974 AH) wrote in his book *As-Sawa'iq Al-Muharraqah fi Rad 'ala Ahlil Bid' wa Zandaqah*:

> Know that what the Ahlus Sunnah wal Jama'ah have consensus that it is obligatory upon every Muslim to purify all the companions by establishing integrity for them and by refraining from reviling them, and by praising them instead. (*As-Sawa'iq*, p208)

Afterwards he mentioned the virtues of the noble companions from the Holy Quran, prophetic Ahadith and the statements of the Salaf; he further wrote:

> And among what is also obligatory upon us is to refrain from mentioning the differences that occurred between them and to turn away from the reports of historians, especially the reports of ignorant Rawafid, misguided Shi'ah and innovators who degrade any of them. (*As-Sawa'iq*, p216)

Moreover he affirmed that it is not enough for events regarding the companions to be quoted in any book, rather we should investigate whether these reports are authentic or not. If something that raises objections on them is established, it is necessary to find a good extrapolation for it and look for the correct explanation of it, as this is what is suitable to the status of the companions. Likewise he said when mentioning the battle between Mu'awiyah and 'Ali ﷺ that the creed of Ahlus Sunnah is that the position of 'Ali ﷺ was correct and he deserves two rewards while Mu'awiyah ﷺ made an error in Ijtihad and he deserves a single reward (*As-Sawa'iq*, p217).

He said the same thing in more detail in *Tathir Al-Jannan wa Al-Lisan 'an Al-Khutur wa At-Tafawuh bi Thalb Saydina Mu'awiyah ibn Abi Sufiyan* (pp. 31, 32, 15), and moreover he said in his book *Az-Zawajir 'an Iqtirab Al-Kaba'ir*:

> The scholars said that when the companions are mentioned in a bad manner such as attributing a defect on them, it is obligatory to refrain from scrutinising such things, rather it is obligatory to reject this with one's hand, then with the tongue and then the heart according to his capacity, like all other evil actions, and this is among the most evil of actions and most repugnant. (*Az-Zawajir*: 2/380-381)

When replying to the objections about Mu'awiyah and 'Amr ibn Abil 'Aas ﷺ, he wrote that whoever examines these events will realise that decisions were taken after discussion and deep thinking, and this is why the Imams of the predecessors and later scholars among the Muslims declared them excused in these wars, because Ali ﷺ and his companions considered them excused as well. Hence there is no place for any Muslim to raise an objection against any of these two groups, rather it is obligatory for every Muslim to hold the creed that Ali ﷺ was the truthful Imam and those fighting him were rebels and both sides are excused and rewarded, and whoever raises any doubt regarding this is a misguided and ignorant person or a stubborn person who deserves no consideration. (*Tathir Al-Jannan*, p38)

THE STATEMENT OF ALLAMAH SHA'RANI

Allamah Abul Mawahib 'AbdulWahab ibn Ahmad Al-Ansari Ash-Sha'rani in his famous book *Al-Yawaqit wa Al-Jawahir,* in the fortieth topic, discussed in particular the conflicts between the companions, and the summary of his statements is as follows:

> It is obligatory to remain silent about the differences which occurred between the noble companions and it is obligatory to believe that they will all be rewarded because by agreement of Ahlus Sunnah, they are all upright, whether one of them participated in these differences and turmoil or not, such as the event of the martyrdom of 'Uthman ﷺ, the disagreement of Mu'awiyah ﷺ, the battle of Jamal, etc. By having a good opinion of them and considering that their actions were based upon Ijtihad, it is obligatory to have such a creed about them, as all these matters were based on Ijtihad, and every Mujtahid is correct or one is correct and the mistaken is excused, rather he deserves a reward. What the biographers have narrated, it does not deserve to be looked at, as it is not authentic and if we suppose it to be authentic, it can have a correct extrapolation. How beautiful is the statement of Umar ibn Abdil Aziz: "Allah has preserved us from this blood so I prefer not to taint my tongue with it." How can reviling and degrading the holders of the religion be allowed? Indeed the one who has reviled the noble companions, he has reviled his religion, and hence the door of revilement should be closed absolutely, especially in discussing the affairs of Mu'awiyah, 'Amr ibn Al-'Aas and companions similar to them ﷺ... (*Al-Yawaqit*: 2/226)

Allamah Sha'rani has the same view as the view of Ahlus Sunnah, that one should refrain from mentioning the conflicts between the companions and their discord, and reviling and blaming them is tantamount to blaming his religion, may Allah protect us from such!

THE STATEMENT OF ALLAMAH MUHIBULLAH

The book *Musallam Ath-Thubut* of Allamah Muhibullah ibn AbdiShakur Al-Bihari (d. 1119 AH) is a famous book of Usul Al-Fiqh which is considered an authority and is part of the curriculum of Arabic Madaris for ages. Allamah Muhibullah says in this book on the topic of the integrity of the companions:

> As for participating in the turmoil, it was based on Ijtihad and acting upon it (Ijtihad) was obligatory by agreement and one cannot be

declared as a corrupt person due to an obligation. (*Musallam Ath-Thubut* with its explanation *Fawatih Ar-Rahmut*: 2/158)

Hence this does not have a single effect on the integrity of the companions. Allamah Muhibullah explained this difficult point with his particular style and the technical terms of Usul Al-Fiqh, and without doubt there is no reply possible to his explanation, but those who have hatred and animosity in their souls against the companions, they cannot be satisfied with any evidence. The sickness of their hearts prevents them from accepting the truth and they are without doubt tested with diseases, and Allah ﷻ said about such diseased people and their disease:

فِى قُلُوبِهِم مَّرَضٌ فَزَادَهُمُ ٱللَّهُ مَرَضًا

In their hearts is disease, so Allah has increased their disease (2: 10).

May Allah preserve us from such!

THE ANALYSIS OF ALLAMAH QURTUBI

The clarification and analysis of Imam Abu Abdillah Muhammad ibn Ahmad Al-Ansari Al-Qutubi (d. 671 AH) regarding the position of Ahlus Sunnah on the disputes between the companions in his famous Tafsir *Al-Jami' li Ahkam Al-Quran* in Surah Al-Hujurat deserves to be consulted. We will present his speech to the readers in a summarised manner:

> It is not permissible to attribute a mistake to a companion in a certain manner because they all practiced Ijtihad in their actions and the aim of all of them was to obtain the satisfaction of Allah ﷻ. All the companions are our Imams and we were ordered to remain silent regarding their internal disputes and to always speak about them in a good manner because of the sanctity of the status of being a companion.

> The Prophet ﷺ forbade us from saying anything bad about them and informed us that Allah ﷻ has forgiven them and He is satisfied with them. With this, it is reported through many chains of narrations that the Messenger of Allah ﷺ said about Talhah ؓ that he is a martyr walking on the earth. So if the going out of Talhah ؓ for fighting against 'Ali ؓ was a sin and disobedience, then a person killed in this conflict would absolutely not reach the status of martyrdom. In the same manner if this action of Talhah ؓ was the result of an error in Ijtihad and was counted as a shortcoming in the performance of an obligatory act, then he would

not have reached the status of martyrdom, as martyrdom is only obtained when someone is killed in the obedience to Allah ﷻ. And this is why it is obligatory to consider their internal disputes upon this creed that we mentioned.

And another proof for this which is famous and authentic and which is reported from by Ali ﷺ himself, is that he said: "The killer of Zubayr will go to hell". Indeed Ali ﷺ said that he heard the Messenger of Allah ﷺ saying: "Give the news of hell to the killer of the son of Saffiyah". So when the matter is such then it is known that Talhah and Zubayr ﷺ are not sinners due to this battle, else the Prophet ﷺ would not have declared Talhah to be a martyr and that the killer of Zubayr will go to hell.

In the same manner, the noble companions who remained away from these fights, they cannot be declared as mistaken in their Ijtihad, rather their actions were correct as well from this perspective and Allah kept their Ijtihad upon this way. When such is the reality then one cannot curse or blame them, disown them and declare them as corrupt and cancel their virtues, Jihad and great religious services. Some scholars were asked about the wars and the blood shed in the battles between the companions, so they in their reply they recited the verse:

$$\text{تِلْكَ أُمَّةٌ قَدْ خَلَتْ لَهَا مَا كَسَبَتْ وَلَكُم مَّا كَسَبْتُمْ وَلَا تُسْئَلُونَ عَمَّا كَانُوا يَعْمَلُونَ}$$

"That is a nation which has passed on. It will have [the consequence of] what it earned, and you will have what you have earned. And you will not be asked about what they used to do." (Al-Baqarah: 141)

Some of them were asked the same and they replied: "This is a blood from which Allah protected my hands, so I wish not to make my tongue sullied with it." They intended to say that they don't want to be tried in declaring any side to be mistaken with certainty... Hasan Al-Basri was also asked about the battles between the companions and he replied: "This was a battle in which the companions were present and I was absent, they were aware of the situation and I was not aware of it. We follow the companions in the matters in which they agree and we remain silent on matters in which they had differences".

Al-Muhasibi said: "We say the same as Hasan Al-Basri; we know that the matters that the companions dealt with, they were more aware of them than us, hence our task is to follow them in matters in which they agreed and to opt for silence in matters in which they differed and we do not invent a new opinion. We are certain that they all exerted

Ijtihad and all desired Allah's closeness, hence they are above any doubt regarding the religion." (*Tafsir Al-Qurtubi*: 16/322)

The analysis of Imam Qurtubi of the tragedic incident that occurred between Ali, Talhah and Zubayr ؓ is thought-provoking; the Prophet ﷺ gave the news of martyrdom for these three as it is narrated through Abu Hurayrah ؓ in *Sahih Muslim* (2/282) and others and these three are among the 10 companions who were given the good news of paradise by the Messenger of Allah ﷺ by name. Ali ؓ declared the killer of Zubayr ؓ to be in hell as it is narrated in *As-Sunnah* of Ibn Abi Asim (2/610), Hakim (3/367) and others, and Hafiz Adh-Dhahabi mentioned it in *As-Siyar* (1/61) and Hafiz Ibn Katheer in *Al-Bidayah* (7/250).

Talhah and Zubayr ؓ requesting Qisas (retaliation) for Uthman ؓ and fighting Ali ؓ over this and finally being martyred in this fight, this is an evidence that their actions were not in pursuit of falsehood; whatever they did, they did it with religiosity and desiring to obtain Allah's satisfaction. Their action against Ali ؓ was not for worldly benefits but based on Ijtihad and difference of opinion and this is why they were declared martyrs on this path. Being promised paradise is something additional, so we should avoid examining these matters deeply and hold a good opinion of them.

THE RULING ON THOSE KILLED

It is attributed to Ali ؓ that he said after the battle of Jamal that the leaders of this battle will be in paradise but those who followed them will go to hell, but Hafiz Dhahabi said:

> The chain of this narration is Mursal and its text contains rejected matters. We seek refuge from Allah from declaring the companions and associates of Zubayr and Mu'awiyah ؓ as going to hell. We leave their matter to Allah and ask for forgiveness for them. (*As-Siyar*: 1/63)

Hence we should not only seek forgiveness for Talhah, Zubayr and Mu'awiyah ؓ but for all of those who took part in the conflicts and battles between the companions; this is the requirement of the verse **"Our Lord, forgive us and our brothers who preceded us in faith..."** (Al-Hashr: 10) as well as the position of all the Salaf.

Contrary to this (Mursal narration), it is narrated from Ali ؓ that he said on the night of Siffin looking in the direction of the people of Shaam: "O

Allah forgive me and them!" (*Ibn Abi Shaybah*: 15/297) And it is narrated with an authentic chain of narration from Yazeed Al-Asam that he asked Ali ﷺ about those killed at Siffin and he replied: "Our killed ones and their killed ones are in paradise" (*Ibn Abi Shaybah*: 15/303; *Majma Zawaid*: 9/357; *Sunan Sa'eed ibn Mansur*: 2/398). This statement of Ali ﷺ with an authentic chain of narration indicates clearly the falsehood of the weak narration mentioned before.

Likewise it is narrated with an authentic chain of narration that 'Amr ibn Sharjeel Abu Maysarah, who was a great worshiper, ascetic and trustworthy personality from Kufah and was counted among the best students of Abdullah ibn Mas'ood, said that he saw in a dream that he was in paradise and he saw beautiful houses. He asked to whom they belonged to and he was told that they belong to Zul Kala' and Hawshab, and these two were with Mu'awiyah ﷺ in the Battle of Siffin and were killed. Abu Maysarah asked where Ammar ﷺ and his companions were and he was told that they are ahead in paradise. He said that these two fought against each other and he was told in reply: "They met Allah and found Him expansive in forgiveness" (*Ibn Abi Shaybah*: 15/290; *Sunan Sa'eed ibn Mansur*: 2/393; *Ibn Sa'd*: 3/264; *As-Sunan Al-Kubra* of Al-Bayhaqi: 8/174; *Al-Ma'rifah wa At-Tarikh*: 3/314; *As-Siyar*: 1/428). Imam Sha'bi said: "They are people of paradise, they met each other and none of them ran away from the other" (*Al-Bidayah*: 7/278).

Umar ibn AbdilAziz said that he saw the Messenger of Allah ﷺ in a dream, Abu Bakr and Umar ﷺ were sitting next to him, he gave them Salam and sat with them. As he sat, Ali and Mu'awiyah ﷺ were brought and they were made to enter a room and its door was closed. While he was looking, Ali ﷺ came out and said: "By the Lord of the Ka'bah, the decision was given in my favour". Then Mu'awiyah ﷺ came out and said: "By the Lord of the Ka'bah, I have been forgiven" (*Al-Bidayah*: 8/130).

These statements and true dreams clarify the position of the Salaf about those who passed away in these conflicts. And this matter is made clear that their internal disputes were not battles between truth and falsehood, between Islam and Kufr, rather it was between truth and closer to the truth, and preponderant over non-preponderant.

Shaykh Al-Islam Ibn Taymiyah writes:

Rather Ali ﷺ was in the end seeking peace and reconciliation with Mu'awiyah ﷺ and refraining from fighting him as Mu'awiyah ﷺ was seeking this at the beginning. So it is known from this that this fight, even if it occurred by Ijtihad, it was not from the sort of fighting whose participants were fighting Allah and His Messenger. (*Minhaj As-Sunnah*: 2/234)

Rather it is also reported from Ali ﷺ that he said about those who remained isolated from these battles that excellence belongs only to the place where Abullah ibn Umar and Sa'd ibn Malik ﷺ stand, if he is good then his reward will be great and if he is bad then his loss will be minimal (*Minhaj As-Sunnah*: 3/180 and 4/180; *Tarikh Al-Islam* of Adh-Dhahabi: 1/553). He ﷺ said to Hasan ﷺ: "Your father didn't know that this matter would linger so much. If only your father had passed away 20 years ago!" (*As-Sunnah* of Ibn Ahmad: 2/555-566; *Minhaj*: 3/180) He also said: "If I knew that this matter would reach such a consequence, I would not have taken such-and-such steps" (*Ibn Abi Shaybah*: 15/293). Likewise he said: "If only my mother did not give me birth! If only I had died before this day" (*At-Tarikh Al-Kabeer* of Al-Bukhari: 6/384).

He ﷺ said when he appointed Abu Musa ﷺ: "Go and free me from this matter even if the veins of my neck are cut - or my neck is cut" (*Athar* of Abu Yusuf, p.208; *Ibn Abi Shaybah*: 15/293). Also "It became clear to Ali ﷺ at the end that the benefit in leaving the fight was greater than in fighting" (*Minhaj*: 2/243) until he even said: "Do not dislike the rule of Mu'awiyah, if it is to be counted on you then you will see heads being separated from fear" (*Minhaj*: 3/180 and others).

These statements of Ali highlight the fact that he was worried at the end, and it was not a confrontation between the truth and falsehood or else he would not be worried about it. And this is why it is reported about these battles that both sides would seek their dead and would bury them together (*Al-Bidayah*: 7/278). Rather Ali would pray their funeral prayers and would say: "Our brothers have revolted against us and the sword cleared their matter" (*Minhaj*: 4/108).

Ammar ﷺ was killed as a martyr while being on the side of Ali ﷺ, and some people, based on the Hadith "The transgressing group will kill him", say vainly that this battle was between the truth and falsehood, but they haven't paid attention absolutely to what Allah ﷻ ordered about the transgressing group. The Qur'an affirms that the transgressing group should be fought to the end but Ali wanted to start peace negotiations and expressed regret after the fight and thought that abandoning fighting was the best option. Hence using this Hadith to say that it was a conflict between truth and falsehood is not correct at all and due to lack of fear of the hereafter.

Like Ali ※, Mu'awiyah ※ was not happy at the situation; his difference with Ali ※ was not based on personal grounds or animosity. Abu Muslim Al-Khawlani said when he asked Mu'awiyah ※ that since he fights Ali, does he think he is better than him? to which Mu'awiyah ※ replied: "No by Allah, I know that Ali is better than me and he deserves the caliphate more than me" (*Aqidah As-Safarini*: 2/328). When Abu Darda and Abu Umamah ※ asked Mu'awiyah ※: "Why do you fight Ali, he became Muslim before you and your father, he is more related to the Prophet ※ than you and he deserves the caliphate more than you?" Mu'awiyah ※ replied: "I am fighting for the blood of Uthman, Ali has given protection to [the killers]. Go to him and tell him that if he gives Qisas (retaliation) to the killers of Uthman, I will be the first from the people of Shaam to give him the pledge of allegiance" (*Al-Bidayah*: 7/260).

Despite his difference with Ali ※, when the Caesar of Rum (Byzantine) wanted to launch an attack taking advantage of the internal battles between the Muslims, Mu'awiyah ※ wrote to him saying:

> By Allah, if you do not cease and return to your country O cursed one, I will certainly do peace with the son of my uncle against you and I will expel you from your country and I will make the earth constrained for you despite its largeness. (*Al-Bidayah*: 8/119; *Taaj Al-Urus*: 7/208)

This letter of Mu'awiyah ※ clearly shows that their internal fight was not based on personal enmity, he would respect Ali ※ and that is why he was saddened by the news of his death. Indeed he said: "Regret be on you! You don't know what people lost from virtue, jurisprudence and knowledge!" (*Al-Bidayah*: 8/130) His crying at the death of Ali ※ is an indication that he regretted his actions. Imam Abdullah ibn Mubarak said that Abdullah ibn Yazeed ibn Asad went to see Mu'awiyah ※ on his death bed and saw that he was crying. He inquired: "O leader of the believers, why are you crying? If you pass away you will go to paradise and if you stay alive, then the people need you?" Mu'awiyah ※ replied: "May Allah have mercy on your father, he would advise me and stop me from killing Hujr ibn Adi" (*Az-Zuhd*: *Al-Isabah*: 6/339); meaning: that at the end he regretted and was worried at the killing of Hujr ibn Adi.

Hafiz Ibn Katheer wrote that in his final moments, Mu'awiyah ※ was asked for a Wasiyah, so he said: "O Allah, forgive my error and overlook my shortcoming, with Your mercy, overlook the naivety of the one whose hope is not linked to other than You. There is no place to run away from You." He said after putting his head on the floor: "O Allah! You said in Your Book that You do not forgive the one who commits polytheism and You forgive besides whomever You want!" (*Al-Bidayah*: 8/142; *As-Siyar*: 3, and others)

All these matters emphasize the fact that Mu'awiyah ﷺ was also worried in the end and sought the forgiveness in the court of his Lord. This clearly shows that his dispute with Ali ﷺ was not for seeking worldly gains; rather whatever he did was based on Ijtihad.

رَبَّنَا ٱغْفِرْ لَنَا وَلِإِخْوَٰنِنَا ٱلَّذِينَ سَبَقُونَا بِٱلْإِيمَٰنِ

Our Lord, forgive us and our brothers who preceded us in faith. (Al-Hashr: 10)

THE POSITION OF IMAM IBN QUDAMAH

Shaykh Al-Islam Imam Muwaffaq Ad-Deen Abu Muhammad Abdullah ibn Ahmad ibn Muhammad ibn Qudamah Al-Maqdisi (d. 620 AH) wrote in his epistle *Lum'ah Al-I'tiqad Al-Hadi ila Sabeel Ar-Rashad* explaining the creed of Ahlus Sunnah:

> The requirement of acting upon the Sunnah is to love and respect the noble companions, to mention their virtues and seek mercy and forgiveness for them, and not to say anything degrading them, to remain silent about the disputes that occurred between them, and with it he should believe that they are the best of this community. (*Lum'ah Al-I'tiqad,* translated edition, p77)

He mentioned afterwards the virtues of the noble companions and pure wives of the Prophet ﷺ and said at the end:

> After the revelation of Ai'shah's ﵂ innocence in the noble Qur'an, if someone accuses her then he is a disbeliever. Mu'awiyah ﷺ is the maternal uncle of all the believers, the writer of the revelation and among the Muslim caliphs. (*Lum'ah,* p79-80)

THE BELIEF OF IMAM ABUL HASAN AL-ASH'ARI

Imam Abul Hasan Ali ibn Isma'eel ibn Ishaq Al-'Ashari (d. 324 AH) was a founder of the knowledge of rhetoric and had reached the level of Ijtihad in the field of knowledge and reason. Among his books whose number is said to reach 300, we count his famous book on creed *Al-Ibanah min Usul Ad-*

Diyanah. He wrote in this book regarding the conflicts between the companions:

> What occurred between Ali, Zubayr and Aishah ﷺ was solely based on Ta'weel (extrapolation) and Ijtihad, and Ali was the Imam and all of them were from the people of Ijtihad; the Prophet ﷺ attested paradise and martyrdom for them, so this indicates that they were upon the truth in their Ijtihad. And likewise what occurred between Ali and Mu'awiyah ﷺ was based on Ta'weel and Ijtihad and all the companions were trustworthy Imams who are not accused in their religion. Indeed Allah and His Messenger ﷺ praised all of them and we were commanded to respect, honour and love them, and we disown anyone who degrades one of them, may Allah have mercy on all of them. (*Al-Ibanah*, pp224-225)

This statement of Imam Ash'ari makes it clear what creed Ahlus Sunnah should hold regarding the companions in general and regarding the internal conflicts in particular. Shaykh Muhammad ibn AbdirRahman Al-Khamees compiled the book *I'tiqad Ahlus Sunnah* with quotes from *Maqalat Imam Ash'ari*. In it, Imam Ash'ari said:

> They know the right of those Allah chose to be the companions of His Prophet ﷺ and they take their virtues, whether small or big, and refrain from mentioning the conflicts that occurred between them.

To explain this statement Shaykh Muhammad ibn AbdirRahman further quoted from *Aqidah Salaf* of Imam Sabuni, *Al-Ibanah* of Imam Ibn Battah, and *I'tiqad Aimah Ahlil Hadith* of Imam Abu Bakr Al-Isma'ili. We have quoted the statements of Imam Sabuni and Imam Ibn Battah in their places. From the statements of these noble scholars, it becomes clear that giving air to the disputes between the companions and making them topics of public discussion is not the way of the Ahlus Sunnah rather a reflection of the thoughts of the Rafidah and Shi'ah.

THE CLEAR STATEMENTS OF MUJADDID ALF THANNI

Shaykh Mujaddid Alf Thani Ahmad Sirhindi clarified the creed of Ahlus Sunnah in many places in his *Maktubat* and it is difficult to quote them in their entirety. Those who desire to read them can consult the details in the first register, second part, Maktub no. 54, 59 and 80; third part, Maktub no. 210;

fourth part, Maktub no. 251, 226; sixth part, Maktub no. 32; seventh part Maktub, no. 67.

We will suffice here to quote some portions from his *Maktubat*. Mujaddid Alf Thanni said:

> May Allah accept the efforts of Ahlus Sunnah! They give a good interpretation of the conflicts and disputes between the companions and they consider them far away from desires of the soul and partisanship because their souls are clean and their chests are definitively pure from animosity and malice due to the effect of accompanying the best of humankind Muhammad ﷺ. In their internal disputes, each of them followed his opinion and Ijtihad and it is obligatory for each of them to act upon his Ijtihad and due to their differences of opinion, disputes and disagreements occurred. Each of them thought it was necessary to act upon his Ijtihad. Their differences of opinion were a spectrum of agreement of the truth and not due to following the desire of the evil soul... The people who had battles with Ali ؓ were a great group of the people of Islam and they had with them great companions and some among them were given the good news of paradise upon the noble tongue of the Prophet ﷺ. So declaring them to be disbelievers and blaming them is not a light matter, the speech that comes of tongues in reviling them is indeed evil, approximately half of the religion and Shari'ah is reported to the community through their mediation, so if they are disparaged or rejected then half of the religion will not be reliable anymore! (Second register, Maktub no. 36)

Likewise he said in another Maktub:

> The differences and conflicts that occurred between the companions were not the result of following one's desires for their desires were according to the Shari'ah. Through their companionship with the best of humankind, their souls became pure and their souls became free of the pollution of the soul commanding evil. Their differences were not based on ignorance but were the result of Ijtihad and knowledge of scholars of truth. Verily Ali ؓ was correct in Ijtihad and the sides opposing him were mistaken, but it was a mistaken Ijtihad which does not lead to Fisq (corruption) so there is no scope even to blame them in these issues, as the mistaken Mujtahid is not a sinner and deserves one reward. Hence one should prevent his tongue from saying anything degrading regarding them and all of them should be remembered with good. One should choose the way of Ahlus Sunnah which is the moderate path between

exaggeration and excess and this is the safest way and the certain path. As for what the commentator of *Mawaqif* quoted, that many of our companions do not believe that these conflicts were based on Ijtihad, then who are these people of knowledge? Contrary to this the creed held by Ahlus Sunnah and which is clearly affirmed in the books of Ahlus Sunnah is that the side opposing Ali ﷺ committed an error in Ijtihad as affirmed by Imam Ghazali, Qadhi Abu Bakr and others, hence declaring them misguided and corrupt is not permissible and no Muslim can dare to say such except if his heart and internal side is polluted with filth. As for some jurists using the word "Jawr" (injustice) for Mu'awiyah ﷺ and declaring him to be a Ja'ir (unjust), what they intended is that during the era of the caliphate of Ali ﷺ, he did not deserve the caliphate and they did not intend the meaning of "Jawr" as corrupt or misguided. This extrapolation has been made so to make this saying according to the creed of Ahlus Sunnah but the people of the right path avoid such words which can give the doubt of being against what is intended, and they do not say anything beyond the word "Khata" (error). How can Mu'awiyah ﷺ be an unjust person when it is established that he would fulfil the rights of Allah and the rights of the Muslims with justice? The words that Shaykh AbdurRahman Jami used, "Khata Munkar" (atrocious error), it is in reality an injustice. Indeed whoever adds to the word "Khata", he would commit an injustice himself. (First register, second part, Maktub no. 54)

Similarly he wrote in another Maktub:

The battles that occurred between the companions, such as the Battle of Jamal or Siffin, we should consider them upon a good interpretation and affirm that they (the companions) were far away from personal desires and biases. These senior companions benefited from the benediction of the company of the Messenger of Allah ﷺ and they were pure from malice and envy. If they kept peace with someone it was only for the truth and if they fought it was only for Allah ﷺ. There is no doubt that each group acted upon his Ijtihad and without any partisanship or personal desire they kept the other far away. Their situation is that the one who is correct will receive two rewards and according to one saying ten rewards and the one who errs will not be deprived of one reward. Moreover the one who erred is far away from any curse or blame in the same manner as the other one (who is right), rather as we said he will deserve at least one reward. Nevertheless the noble scholars said that in the wars, the position of Ali ﷺ was right and his opponents erred in

Ijtihad and they cannot be criticised and nor is there scope for any blame upon them, so what is to be said about imputing disbelief or Fisq (corruption) on them? Ali ﷺ himself said about them: "They are our brothers, they rebelled against us." They are neither disbelievers nor corrupt, as their difference was based on extrapolation which is a preventive factor (Mani') of disbelief and corruption. Our Prophet ﷺ told us to avoid entering into the differences between his companions; hence we should respect and honour all the companions and remember them all with good words, and one should not have a bad suspicion about any of them. This is the path of salvation and success because love of the companions is because of the Messenger of Allah ﷺ. One of the saints said: "The one who did not respect and honour the companions, he did not have faith in the Messenger of Allah ﷺ. (Second Register, Maktub no. 67)

The excellent manner in which these words of Mujaddid Alf Thani clarified the position of Ahlus Sunnah regarding the conflict between the companions leaves no scope for any doubt for people of pure natural disposition. This also makes it clear that the views of some scholars who rushed in these matters and used inappropriate words, were their personal views and absolutely not a reflection of the view of Ahlus Sunnah. Mujaddid Alf Thani wrote a separate epistle against the Rawafid entitled *Rad Ar-Rawafid* and he mentioned in it the same position as the one expressed in *Maktubat*. This epistle has been translated in Arabic and was published in 141/1991 in Istanbul.

What Mujaddid Alf Thanni said regarding the statement of the commentator of *Al-Mawaqif* who said: "A great number of our scholars of the Sunnah declare those who fought Ali ﷺ as Fasiq (corrupt)" deserves to be noted. Indeed who are these scholars of the Sunnah and what is their number? Whereas we found the position of the scholars of Sunnah from the first century up untill the present to be contrary to this. Readers had the opportunity to read the quotes from reliable books of creed and the statements of the four jurists and scholars of Hadith have also been presented, so then we can ask: Who are the "great number of scholars of the Sunnah" in opposition to all of them?

It is extremely regrettable that some people tried to advocate the commentator of *Al-Mawaqif,* Allamah Sayed Shareef Ali ibn Muhammad Al-Jurjani and tried to find one or two statements of this kind to justify that those who fought against Ali ﷺ were Fasiq (corrupt) and that their fight was not based on an error in Ijtihad. With great celerity, they quoted the statement of

Ammar ibn Yasir ﷺ present in *As-Sunnan Al-Kubra* (8/174) wherein he said: "Do not say that the people of Shaam have committed disbelief but they committed Fisq or injustice", while taking evidence from the statement of one side against the other in these internal disputes is wrong.

Abbas and Ali ﷺ differed concerning the inheritance of the Prophet ﷺ, Abbas said in front of Umar Farooq ﷺ and a group of companions that Ali ﷺ was a liar, sinner and treacherous (*Muslim*: 2/90), so would it be correct to have such an opinion about Ali ﷺ? We seek refuge from Allah from the evil of our souls.

It is also narrated from Ammar that he said: "Do not declare the people of Shaam to be disbelievers, our Prophet is the same, our Qiblah is the same, rather they are people who have been captivated in a turmoil (Qawmun Maftunun)" (*Ibn Abi Shaybah*: 15/290-291). but you have read the statement of Imam Abdullah ibn Mubarak: "The sword which ran among the companions was a Fitnah (trial, turmoil) and I do not say about any of them that they were Maftun (captivated in the Fitnah)" (*As-Siyar*: 8/405); you can see the precaution of the Salaf and their respect towards the companions, and how nowadays their speech against each other is used as evidence to declare them Fasiq (corrupt) or misguided, *Inna Lillahi wa Inna ilayhi Rajiun* (We all belong to Allah and to Him we will return)! Hence the statement of the commentator of *Al-Mawaqif* or any other scholar can be his personal opinion, but it cannot in any way be declared as the opinion of Ahlus Sunnah as clarified by Mujaddid Alf Thanni and many other scholars.

THE VERDICT OF ALLAMAH TAFTAZANI

Allamah Sa'd Ad-Din Mas'ood ibn Umar Taftazani (d. 792 AH) is a famous Imam of Usul Al-Fiqh and a jurist. In the field of creed, his book *Sharh Al-'Aqaid* is famous and it is included in Arabic Madaris. He mentioned in it regarding the companions:

> And one should refrain from mentioning the companions except with good due to the authentic Prophetic narrations about their virtues and the obligation of refraining from blaming them... And as for the battles and disputes that occurred between them, it has explanations and extrapolations. (*Sharh Al-'Aqaid* with *An-Nibras*, pp546, 549)

THE STATEMENT OF ALLAMAH AS-SAFARINI

The Muhadith of Shaam Imam Muhammad ibn Ahmad ibn Salim As-Saffarini (d. 1188 AH) discussed this topic in detail in his book *Ad-Durrah Al-Madhiyah* and its explanation *Sharh Lawamih Al-Anwar Al-Bahiyah*. He said:

> The disputes, arguments and fights that occurred between the noble companions were based on Ijtihad between the leaders of both sides. The aim of each side was correct though only one side was upon the truth and it was Ali ﷺ and his companions, and those who opposed him were mistaken but the mistaken side will obtain one reward; only the people of aversion and hatred differ about this. It is obligatory to interpret the authentic narrations about the conflicts of the companions in a good manner in a way that it removes accusations of sins upon them. Hence the harsh speech that occurred between Ali and Abbas ﷺ did not bring a defect to any of them. Likewise Ali ﷺ did not give the pledge of allegiance to Abu Bakr ﷺ at the beginning due to one of these two reasons: either because he was not consulted as he complained about it himself or it was in support of Fatimah ﷺ who believed that she deserved a portion of the Prophet's inheritance; then without any doubt he gave pledge of allegiance to Abu Bakr ﷺ in front of everyone and by Allah's grace they were all united and their aim was fulfilled.
>
> Likewise when Ali ﷺ paused before taking Qisas (retaliation) for Uthman ﷺ, it was to know the culprits with certainty and he thought that if he takes Qisas in such conditions, it will increase the turmoil. Aishah, Talhah, Zubayr and Mu'awiyah ﷺ opposed him and considered that it was permissible for them to fight Ali ﷺ, and some of them were Mujtahid and some followed their leaders, and the people of truth agree that Ali ﷺ was upon the truth in these battles. And the correct creed which cannot be compromised is that all the companions were upright and they exercised extrapolation and Ijtihad in these battles, hence for the people of truth, the truth is one but the one who makes efforts to reach the truth and does not have any shortcoming in this, even after a mistake he will deserve a reward and will not be sinful.
>
> There were ambiguous matters in these battles and confusion was so severe that the views of the companions differed regarding them and they became divided into three groups: A group's Ijtihad reached the conclusion that one side should be helped and the opposing side is rebellious, hence for them it was obligatory to help the rightful side and fight the rebellious group and they acted accordingly and it is clear for

someone who reached such a conclusion that it was absolutely not right to have any shortcoming in helping the Imam and fighting the rebels.

The second group was opposing this one and what is said about the first group applies to them.

The third group of companions could not arrive at a decision and they could not decide which side was preponderant so this group remained isolated and they believed that isolating from both sides was obligatory upon them as fighting a Muslim is not permissible until a religious evidence becomes manifest to them.

The conclusion is that all these groups were excused and will be rewarded and not be sinful. And this is why the scholars of the people of truth agree on the fact that their testimonies and narrations are accepted and they are all upright. And this is why the scholars of our country, rather all of Ahlus Sunnah among whom we count Ibn Hamdan (the author of *Nihayah Al-Mubtadi'in*) said that it was obligatory to love all the companions and avoid writing, reading, teaching and hearing the events that occurred between them, and it is obligatory to mention their virtues, express satisfaction and love of them, abandon blaming them, consider them excused and have the certitude that whatever they did was based on Ijtihad which does not lead to disbelief or Fisq (corruption) but rather they will be rewarded on some instances due to their Ijtihad.

Some people said that the truth was with Ali ﷺ and those who fought him will be forgiven. What the author of the poem *Ad-Durrah Al-Madhiyah* said about not deeply analysing the conflicts is because Imam Ahmad would blame those who would scrutinise (these conflicts), and he would accept their virtues mentioned in Ahadith and he would disown those who declared the companions as disbelievers or misguided and he would say that the correct way is to remain silent regarding the conflicts between the companions. (*Lawaih Al-Anwar Al-Bahiyah*: 2/369-370)

Likewise he said in *Lawamih Al-Anwar* (1/46) after mentioning the virtues of the companions:

It is obligatory upon the people to mention their excellent qualities, remain silent about their internal disputes and consider such differences as the result of their Ijtihad, that whatever each side did, they considered it as obligatory for them and better for the religion, and each Mujtahid will receive the reward for his action.

After this detailed explanation of Allamah As-Saffarini, there remains no difficulty in understanding the position of Ahlus Sunnah that one should respect the noble companions and express love towards them and no words should be uttered about them that can indicate lack of respect. One should remain silent regarding their conflicts and interpret their disputes as differences in Ijtihad.

With his speech, two matters are necessary to be mentioned in a concise manner. The first is that he said that according to the known saying, Ali ﷺ gave pledge of allegiance to Abu Bakr ﷺ after the death of Fatimah ﷺ but it is based on the speech of Imam Zuhri which is Mursal, while it is narrated with an authentic chain of narration that Ali ﷺ gave the pledge of allegiance to Abu Bakr ﷺ in the Prophetic Mosque along with the general public as it has been narrated by Imam Bayhaqi in *Al-I'tiqad* (p178); *As-Sunan Al-Kubra*: 8/143; Imam Hakim in *Al-Mustadrak*: 3/76, and as quoted by Hafiz Ibn Katheer in *Al-Bidayah*: 5/248-249 and 6/302. Imam Bayhaqi and Hafiz Ibn Katheer declared it to be authentic and preponderant; also see *As-Sunan Al-Kubra*: 6/300; Hafiz Ibn Hajar also mentioned it from Ibn Hibban and said that he gave a second pledge of allegiance after six months to remove doubts, and one can read the details of it in *Fath Al-Bari* (7/495, Bab Ghazwah Khaybar, no. 4241).

The second matter, Allamah As-Saffarini's statement that those who remained isolated from the battles of Jamal and Siffin could not reach a decision hence they remained isolated, is questionable and what is correct is that they remained isolated due to many texts and this has been clarified before in a concise manner.

THE VERDICT OF IMAM AL-HIND SHAH WALIYULLAH

The importance of the book *Izalah Al-Khafa 'An Khilafah Al-Khulafa* by the Imam of India Shah Waliyullah Muhadith Dehlwi is not hidden to any person of knowledge. Shah Waliyullah wrote regarding the conflicts between the companions in his particular style:

> Aishah, Talhah and Zubayr ﷺ were mistaken and excused due to the principle that the Mujtahid who errs deserves a reward. So they were excused as they took evidence from a doubt though there was a stronger proof. And the reasons of this doubt were two matters...

Afterwards he mentioned these two doubts and mentioned the evidences and corroborative facts for them, and it is not necessary to mention them here in detail. After this, Shah Waliyullah affirmed that the Battle of Siffin between Mu'awiyah and Ali ﷺ was based on the same doubts. He said:

> Mu'awiyah ﷺ was a Mujtahid who erred and is excused, and the reason of it is that he took evidence on a doubt though there was an evidence heavier in the scale of the Shari'ah, in the same manner as we have mentioned in the story of Al-Jamal with the additions of more variables here.

Meaning: Mu'awiyah ﷺ had more complex matters than the people of Al-Jamal and due to these he could not give pledge of allegiance to Ali ﷺ which resulted in the Battle of Siffin. Due to the complex nature of these matters, Mu'awiyah ﷺ was excused though the position of Ali ﷺ was more preponderant and correct from the perspective of evidences. Those who want to be acquainted with these more complex matters can read them in *Izalah Al-Khafa*, because mentioning these issues in detail here is not the aim and will make this book longer.

THE POSITION OF QADHI THANAULLAH PANIPATI

The Bayhaqi of his time, Qadhi Thanaullah Panipati (d. 1225 AH), the famous student of Shah Waliyullah Dehlwi, replied with seriousness to the objections against the noble companions in his book *As-Sayf Al-Maslool* and he clarified that the conflicts between them were based on Ijtihad. He wrote:

> The chapter "Rad Mata'in 'an As-Sahabah" has clarified that the internal disputes and battles between the noble companions were based on errors in Ijtihad and it does not prove the disbelief of any party. Indeed the leader of the believers Ali ibn Abi Talib ﷺ said: "We fought our Muslim brothers because they were wrong headed and had misapprehension and the doubt of extrapolation." The Messenger of Allah ﷺ said about Hasan ﷺ: "This son of mine is a leader, maybe through him Allah will reconcile two great factions among the Muslims". Hence the conflicts of Mu'awiyah and Amr ibn Aas ﷺ do not prevent them from being companions of the Messenger ﷺ, for these nobles were companions of the Messenger ﷺ and their superiority and greatness over non-companions is necessary according to general texts from the Book and the Sunnah, even if this greatness was bigger than the distance

> between the throne of Allah and the ground of the earth. And this is why all the companions should be remembered with good and we should invoke for them, we should not have any rancour or animosity, we should keep our tongues silent about the conflicts between them, , and it is appropriate to do good extrapolations of them. (*As-Sayf Al-Maslool*, translated edition, pp484-485)

Likewise after refuting the eighth objection of the Rawafid, he wrote:

> Having enmity towards the companions after neglecting many of their virtues, and blaming them by only focusing on a few events, amounts to have enmity towards the religion. If a statement or action is established from them which seems to oppose the Shari'ah, one should extrapolate it or have a good opinion about them as the testimony of goodness for this group has been established by the Shari'ah. (*As-Sayf Al-Maslool*, p380)

SIRAJ AL-HIND SHAH ABDULAZIZ MUHADITH DEHLWI

The book *Izalah Al-Khafa 'an Khilafah Al-Khulafa* of Shah Waliyullah Muhadith Dehlwi had a great influence in refuting the turmoil of Rafd and Shiism. His students played a great role in spreading his mission, and the books As-*Sayf Al-Maslool* by Qadhi Thanaullah Panipati and *Tuhfah Ithna Ashariyah* of his son, the Imam of the scholars, Siraj Al-Hind Shah Abdul Aziz Muhadith Dehlwi (d. 1239 AH) constitute a golden chain on this issue. In the twelfth chapter of *Tuhfah Ithna Ashariyah*, after refuting the objections of the Rafidis, he clarified the position of Ahlus Sunnah that the differences among the companions with Ali ﷺ on issues such as Imamah, the issue of Hibah (gift), the distribution of the fifth of the booty, Mut'ah Al-Hajj and others were due to Ijtihad. In the same manner as Ali ﷺ was a Mujtahid, the companions who differed with him were also Mujtahid and it is permissible to differ in matters of Ijtihad, it does not deserve refutation or blame. Those who fought Ali ﷺ with hatred such as Khawarij, then they are disbelievers in the ruling of the hereafter by consensus of Ahlus Sunnah, hence it is not allowed to seek forgiveness for them. He said:

> By analogy to this, those who fought Ali ﷺ not due to hatred but due to false extrapolation such as those who took part in the Battle of Jamal and Siffin, their mistake was common (Mushtarak) to error in Ijtihad and falsehood of creed, but the difference is that error in Ijtihad and corruption in creed (Fisq I'tiqadi) does not make the people of Jamal

deserving of any blame and degradation because decisive texts and Mutawatir Ahadith are praising them, they are related to the Prophet ﷺ through blood and marriage, they are very close to him and from the first forerunners. Their differences and disputes are of the same kind as the difference from Musa عليه السلام and Harun عليه السلام. There are certain texts established on the greatness of Musa عليه السلام and they are preventive factors from blaming him from what he did to his elder brother. Indeed, whatever he did, he did it for Allah's sake and not by being affecting by a touch of the devil. And these matters are also absolutely not established for the people of Siffin, hence being silent about them is obligatory due to the general verses and Ahadith revealed about the companions rather about all the people of faith, one should hope for success and forgiveness for them. (*Tuhfah*, p626)

We have not quoted the Persian quote completely to make it concise, though we quoted the summary of it in our words. One should not be worried by the words "Fisq I'tiqadi" used by Shah AbdulAziz as he himself clarified: "In the custom (Urf) of Ahlus Sunnah an error in Ijtihad is synonymous to Fisq I'tiqadi" (*Tuhfah*, p618). Likewise he wrote clearly:

> The major companions, the mother of the believers ﵂ in particular, did not intend to fight the leader of the believers Ali ﵇; their aim was to take Qisas (retaliation) from the killers of Uthman ﵇... And it is apparent that they did not have any hatred towards Ali ﵇ and their fight was not based on animosity but rather to remove corruption and taking Qisas for Uthman ﵇. (p623)

Shah AbdulAziz Dehlwi clarified in principal the position of Ahlus Sunnah in an excellent manner; that the companions' fights were based on Ijtihad and the position of one side was erroneous and their extrapolation was not correct, yet we cannot blame any side and we should remain silent about it. It is very regrettable that despite all the clear statements of the Salaf and those of Shah AbdulAziz Dehlwi and his father, some are daring to trying to prove that the fight of Mu'awiyah against Ali ﵇ was not based on Ijtihad. They are relying on one or two statements of Shah AbdulAziz without any basis and it is not the place to discuss this in detail, while you have read the speech of the Salaf in great detail about the doubts that Aishah, Mu'awiyah and others ﵀ had in the conflict against Ali ﵇, and according to Shah Waliyullah, Mu'awiyah ﵇ was facing more complexities. And consider the reason why they declare Mu'awiyah ﵇ and others as mistaken while Abdullah ibn Umar ﵇ did not give pledge of allegiance to Ali ﷺ but at the end he gave pledge of allegiance to Mu'awiyah ﷺ and accepted him as the leader, who will they at the end declare as mistaken?

THE POSITION OF ALLAMAH PARHARI

The scholar who had the same first name and lived in the same era of Shah Abdul Aziz Muhadith Dehlwi, Allamah Abu AbdirRahman Abdul Aziz Qureshi Parhari (d. 1239 AH) was from the village Parharan Kot in the area of Muzaffarabad. He was born and buried in this village and lived for 33 years but he authored in this young age more than 30 books (*Fuqaha e Hind*, p100, 13th Century AH).

You have read previously what Allamah Taftazani said in *Sharh Aqa'id*, and Allamah Abdul Aziz wrote in its explanation:

> And the explanation is that they were seeking the truth but some were correct in their Ijtihad and others erred in Ijtihad but they will not be taken to account rather will be rewarded. Thus was the habit of the pious predecessors, they would give a good meaning to the actions of the companions. (*An-Nibras*, p549)

Allamah Abdul Aziz wrote a separate epistle in the defence of Mu'awiyah entitled *An-Nihayah 'an Ta'n Ameer Al-Muminin Mu'awiyah*. He said in it:

> Many of the verifying scholars said that mentioning them (the conflicts between the companions) is forbidden fearing that it would lead to having bad opinion about some of the companions. (*An-Nihayah*, p5)

He wrote in the same epistle:

> Verily our school of thought of Ahlus Sunnah wal Jama'ah is to display efforts in extrapolating the (conflicts) and when extrapolating is not possible, it is obligatory to reject such narrations, remain silent and refrain from raising any blame on them. (*An-Nihayah*, p33)

THE STATEMENT OF NAWAB SIDDIQ HASAN KHAN

The efforts of Shaykh Nawab Siddiq Hasan Qanuji (d. 1307 AH) in India and his plethora of writings are not hidden to the people of knowledge. Nawab Siddiq Hasan Khan wrote when explaining the creed of Ahlus Sunnah:

From the fundamentals of Ahlus Sunnah wal Jama'ah is they keep their tongues safe from reviling the companions of the Messenger of Allah ﷺ... And they refrain from mentioning the conflicts between them... (*Qatf Ath-Thamar fi Bayan Aqeedah Ahlil Thamar,* pp97-103)

So having any kind of bad feeling in his heart towards the companions, having suspicion about them instead of having a good opinion of them, mentioning their disputes with great enthusiasm and making such a topic of public discourse is not the behaviour of Ahlus Sunnah rather a sign of the people of innovation.

THE FATWA OF SHAYKH AL-KULL MIAN NAZEER HUSAYN MUHADITH DEHLWI

The inheritor of the chair of Shah Waliyullah Muhadith Dehlwi and the successor of Shah Muhammad Ishaq Muhadith Dehlwi, Shaykh Al-Kull Mian Nazeer Husayn Dehlwi (d. 1320 AH) wrote a detailed Fatwa which is present among his *Fatawa*; a person asked whether it was permissible to call Mu'awiyah ؓ a rebel or mistaken when mentioned against Ali ؓ or not? And whether it was necessary to mention him as Ameer, Imam or say: "Radhi Allah anhu" (May Allah be pleased with him)" when mentioning him alone, not against Ali ؓ, and the error that Ameer Mu'awiyah ؓ did, did he expiate it or not, and if someone out of bigotry only says Mu'awiyah, what is the ruling on him? Molvi Muhammad Fasih Ghazipuri first gave the answers to these questions, and the summary of his answers is that when Ameer Mu'awiyah is mentioned against Ali ؓ, in such places the word "Hazrat" or saying any invocation is not correct, though one should not say bad words about him and one should keep his tongue silent from such. Mu'awiyah ؓ rebelled against a rightly guided caliph, hence we should consider him as mistaken and a rebel, and if his mistake or rebellion was removed, why would the scholar declare him to be mistaken and rebel, and when mentioning him alone, not against Ali ؓ, then "Hazrat" should be said as he was a companion of the Messenger of Allah ﷺ.

When these answers were presented to Mian Nazeer Husayn Dehlwi, he refuted them and mentioned the position of Ahlus Sunnah with great clarity, and more than a dozen of scholars supported the Fatwa of Mian Nazeer Husayn Dehlwi and declared it to be correct. These questions and answers are in Persian, present in *Fatawa Nazeeriyah* (3/445-456 for around 12 pages); we will mention here its summary:

It is not hidden to the people of intellect and sincerity that Ameer Mu'awiyah ﷺ is a companion of the Messenger of Allah ﷺ. Ibn Battal narrated with an authentic chain of narration from Ibn Abbas that he said that the Messenger of Allah ﷺ said not to insult his companions, their sitting with the Prophet ﷺ is better than 40 years of your actions, and Wakee's narration says better than the actions of your whole life.

Mu'awiyah ﷺ became Muslim at the conquest of Makkah and he narrated 163 Ahadith in the Sihhah Sittah and other books. Many major companions narrated from him such as Abdullah ibn Abbas, Abdullah ibn Umar, Abdullah ibn Zubayr, Abu Darda, Jarir ibn Abdillah Al-Bajali, Nu'man ibn Basheer and others ﷺ, and among the Tabi'un we count Sa'eed ibn Al-Musayyab, Humayd ibn AbdirRahman and others. It is narrated in *Sahih Al-Bukhari* that Mu'awiyah ﷺ prayed one Rak'ah Witr, the servant of Abdullah ibn Abbas ﷺ was near and he went to inform Ibn Abbas ﷺ that Mu'awiyah ﷺ prayed only one Rak'ah of Witr, and he replied that he is "a companion of the Messenger of Allah ﷺ," and in another version that he acted correctly and he is a jurist companion, so it is established in *Sahih Al-Bukhari* that he is a companion and according to Ibn Abbas ﷺ, he is upright and a jurist, so he deserves to be invoked for Allah to be pleased with him and bestow on Him mercy as according to Ahlus Sunnah, saying "Radhiya Allah anhu" (may Allah be pleased with him) is recommended by agreement, so by his status of being a companion, when he is mentioned against Ali ﷺ, using the words "Hazrat" and "Radhia Allah Anhu" is recommended and not forbidden as mutual fights do not deprive companions from their status of being companions while the school of though of Rafidah is contrary to this.

Though there is a big difference of level between Ameer Mu'awiyah and Ali ﷺ as Ali is among the 10 promised with paradise, he has a lengthy companionship, and he is the son-in-law of the Prophet ﷺ. So saying "may Allah be pleased with him" for a companion and "may Allah have mercy on him" for Tabi'un and those after them is recommended. Other than the companions, however great they are, cannot reach the level of companions as the status of companionship entails many rights. Mu'awiyah ﷺ is a companion; hence he is better than all non-companions on the surface of the earth, even though the difference among the companions is greater than the distance from the throne of Allah to the ground of the earth. And this is why we should remember them in a good manner and not have any rancour and enmity in our hearts towards them, we should have in our hearts as much love as they had for the Prophet ﷺ.

And those who fought among the companions, it was due to error in Ijtihad and no one is declared disbeliever for an error in Ijtihad. Indeed Ali ؓ himself affirmed that we are "fighting our Muslims brothers as they have a doubt and an extrapolation which generated misapprehension in their hearts," and the Messenger of Allah ﷺ said about Hasan: "This son of mine is a leader, maybe through him Allah will reconcile two great factions among the Muslims".

It is mentioned in *As-Sayf Al-Maslool* of Qadhi Thanaullah Panipati, *Nahj Al-Azhar* of Mulla Ali Qari, and *Tuhfah Ithna Ashariyah* of Shah AbdulAziz that it is written in a Mutawatir way in the book of the Shi'ah that Ali ؓ forbade to curse the people of Shaam and affirmed that "we are fighting our brothers as their hearts had apprehension due to doubt and extrapolation." Shaykh AbdulQadir Jilani said that Ahlus Sunnah agree that one should refrain his tongue from mentioning the disputes between the companions and anything bad about them (we have quoted his complete speech before). This statement of the beloved of Allah Shaykh Jilani makes it clear that the battles between the companions were due to Ijtihad, we should remain silent about them and leave their matter to Allah ﷻ. The people who died on both sides are martyrs as both of them believed they were upon the truth though in reality one group was upon the truth and the other was mistaken and this mistake was Ijtihad, which is forgiven by Allah ﷻ.

It was asked in the questions that if someone considers himself to be among Ahlus Sunnah and out of bigotry does not say "May Allah be pleased" for Mu'awiyah ؓ but rather speaks evil about him, what is his ruling? Then the answer is: Ameer Mu'awiyah ؓ fought Ali ؓ and Ali was right in this fight and Ameer Mu'awiyah was mistaken, and according to Ahlus Sunnah it is not permissible to insult, revile or have a bad opinion of him due to this mistake in Ijtihad, rather it is not even permissible to curse a particular corrupt person or someone doing major sins. And one can not even say anything bad about someone who erred in Ijtihad, so if anyone due to bigotry and hatred does not say "May Allah be pleased with him", then he is under the threat mentioned in the Hadith, for verily the Messenger of Allah ﷺ said not to revile his companions and that the curse of Allah is on whoever reviles his companions, insults them and says evil about them.

And such a person is a hidden Rafidi though he manifests himself as being from Ahlus Sunnah. Likewise the unfortunate who speaks evil about Aishah Siddiqah ﷢, in reality he tries to harm Allah and His Messenger ﷺ. It is necessary for the one who holds a bad creed regarding his noble wife and noble companions to repent and opt for the school of thought of Ahlus Sunnah. To be part of Ahlus Sunnah, one should believe about the companions that regarding the four guided caliphs, their level and status is according to the order (of their caliphate), and one should believe in the virtue mentioned about each companion in authentic Ahadith and in the creed of Ahlus Sunnah. And the details of this is mentioned in *Sharh Mawaqif, Sharh Maqasid,* and *Izalah Al-Khafa* so one can consult them and remove his ignorance and come out of his naivety and know the school of thought of Ahlus Sunnah. (*Fatawa Nazeeriyah*, pp445-456)

We are completing our epistle on this, or else if we were to mention the scholars after and their statements, it will not double the size of this book, but reach many volumes. This makes the matter clear as day light that one should refrain from mentioning anything bad regarding the companions, and we, by considering their internal disputes as within the circles of Ijtihad, should not delve and scrutinise this issue and avoid mentioning such events in front of laymen, as this way can lead them to revile and criticise the noble companions and they might have suspicion and a bad creed about them, and their sanctity and nobility might be affected by such, and instead of love and good opinion, the person will develop bad opinion, and this was the view of Ahlus Sunnah since the first generation up to now. May Allah keep us steadfast upon this and give us the favour of loving and honouring the noble companions!

رَبَّنَا ٱغْفِرْ لَنَا وَلِإِخْوَٰنِنَا ٱلَّذِينَ سَبَقُونَا بِٱلْإِيمَٰنِ وَلَا تَجْعَلْ فِى قُلُوبِنَا غِلًّا لِّلَّذِينَ ءَامَنُوا۟

رَبَّنَآ إِنَّكَ رَءُوفٌ رَّحِيمٌ

Our Lord, forgive us and our brothers who preceded us in faith and put not in our hearts [any] resentment toward those who have believed. Our Lord, indeed You are Kind and Merciful. (Al-Hashr: 10)

Ameen, O Lord of the universe!

Irshad Al-Haqq Al-Athari

9 798555 240064